Microwave Cooking

JUDITH R. KNORR
Writer

BARBARA FELLER-ROTH
Editor

KEITH OVREGAARD
Photographer

STEPHANIE GREENLEIGH
Food Stylist

FELICIA SALA SNOW
Photographic Stylist

Judith R. Knorr, a free-lance home economist and high school home economics teacher, has lectured and taught extensively on microwave cooking. A graduate of Ohio University with a degree in home economics, she has been a consultant for appliance and cookware manufacturers, and a Cooperative Extension Advisor for the United States Department of Agriculture in Illinois. Her food articles appear in magazines and newspapers across the country. She lives with her husband and two sons in Huntington, New York.

The California Culinary Academy In the forefront of American institutions leading the culinary renaissance in this country, the California Culinary Academy in San Francisco has gained a reputation as one of the most outstanding professional chef training schools in the world. With a teaching staff recruited from the best restaurants of Western Europe, the Academy educates students from around the world in the preparation of classical cuisine. The recipes in this book were created in consultation with the chefs of the Academy. For information about the Academy, write the Office of the Dean, California Culinary Academy, 625 Polk Street, San Francisco, CA 94102.

Front Cover
Serve Lemon-Mint Lamb Chops (see page 77), appetizingly seared on a microwave browning dish, with tender new potatoes and green beans. Garnish Blueberry-Lemon Mousse Parfaits (see page 98) with fresh blueberries, lemon zest, and whipped cream for an elegant finish to the meal.

Title Page
Thread marinated chicken cubes, mushroom caps, chunks of bell pepper, cherry tomatoes, and whole white onions on microwave-safe skewers and cook on a microwave-safe rack for a Teriyaki Chicken Kabob dinner (see page 73) that doesn't look like conventional microwave fare.

Back Cover
Upper Left: Pick herbs fresh from the garden and dry them quickly in the microwave oven for a year-round supply.
Upper Right: The very sweet filling in Rich Butterscotch Tarts (see page 98) makes them an ideal ending to an elegant light meal.
Lower Left: Make Vegetable-Stuffed Cabbage Rolls (see page 53) the star of a vegetarian dinner; they're filled with Cheddar and cream cheese, broccoli, mushrooms, carrots, onion, zucchini, and garlic.
Lower Right: Four Cornish game hens are arranged artfully on a platter with baby carrots and green beans. Among the lessons to be learned from professional chefs is that the way food is presented is as important as how it tastes.
Special Thanks To Ruth Roush, Rosemary Matheson, Ocean Fresh Seafood, Panasonic Company, Cottonwood, Best of All Worlds, Cookin, Andrea Cypress, David J. Knorr, Paul Knorr, Kent Knorr.

Contributors

Calligraphers
Keith Carlson, Chuck Wertman

Additional Photographers
Laurie Black, at the Academy, pages 6, 32, 43, and 101
Alan Copeland, at the Academy, pages 74, 93, 98, 112, 118, and 121
Kit Morris, CCA chefs, below left
Davide China, author, at left
Barbara and Richard Tauber, pages 10, 13, 44, 69, 116, 119, and 122

Additional Food Stylist
Randy Mon

Photographic Design Consultant
Debbie Dicker

Copy Chief
Melinda E. Levine

Editorial Coordinator
Cass Dempsey

Copyeditor
Toni Murray

Proofreader
Leslie Cole

Indexer
Elinor Lindheimer

Editorial Assistants
Andrea Y. Connolly, Karen K. Johnson, Tamara Mallory

Composition & pagination by
Linda M. Bouchard, Robert C. Miller, Laurie Prather

Series format design by
Linda Hinrichs, Carol Kramer

Production by
Studio 165

Separations by
Color Tech Corp.

Lithographed in U.S.A. by
Webcrafters, Inc.

The California Culinary Academy series is produced by the staff of Ortho Information Services.

Publisher
Robert J. Dolezal

Editorial Director
Christine Robertson

Production Director
Ernie S. Tasaki

Series Managing Editor
Sally W. Smith

System Manager
Katherine L. Parker

Address all inquiries to
Ortho Information Services
Box 5047
San Ramon, CA 94583

Chevron Chemical Company
6001 Bollinger Canyon Road
San Ramon, CA 94583

TX
832
.K65
1988

C O N T E N T S

Microwave Cooking

For a delightful quick breakfast, serve scrambled eggs and bacon (see recipes on page 34) and Cinnamon Crumb Muffins (page 33), all made in the microwave.

Introduction to Microwave Cooking

The microwave oven has been hailed as the first new method of cooking since fire. It's fast, easy, and produces fabulous, fresh-tasting food. This book provides a wealth of delicious recipes and menus, cooking methods, and helpful tips to introduce you to microwave cooking. Included in this chapter is an easy-to-understand explanation of how microwave ovens work, so you can learn the most efficient use of your oven. Be sure to read Timing a Microwave Meal (see page 7) for hints on turning out several dishes at the same time.

ABOUT MICROWAVE OVENS

Welcome to microwave cooking. You are entering the newest facet of the world of cookery. Your microwave oven probably seems like a combination of a new toy and a tool of the future. Actually it is both. It's something new that you will learn to operate and it is definitely a cooking mode of the future. The phenomenal growth in sales of microwave ovens is ensuring the existence of a microwave in the kitchen of tomorrow.

Some microwave cooking methods are different from those of conventional cooking; these differences are covered in this chapter. In addition to familiarizing yourself with them, read the use and care booklet provided by the manufacturer of your microwave oven. Because it is written for the model of oven that you have, it should answer any specific questions that may be raised in the general information presented here.

Take the time to learn to operate the microwave oven correctly. Be relaxed and ready to learn. You will soon find your microwave one of the most valuable tools in your kitchen.

A microwave oven will not automatically make you a better cook. Although it will help you prepare meals faster, the food will not be any better than the ingredients you select, the good sense you use, and the flair you incorporate into the recipes you choose. Prepare the recipes in the following chapters, make substitutions to fit your family tastes, and most of all enjoy your microwave and all it can do for you.

How Microwave Ovens Work

Microwaves accomplish the following in a microwave oven: excite molecules, pass through certain materials, and reflect off certain materials. Microwaves that strike water, fat, or sugar molecules cause the molecules to jiggle rapidly and rub against each other. The friction produces heat sufficient to cook the food. Microwaves pass through glass, plastic, and paper because these materials have no water, fat, or sugar molecules. Microwaves reflect or bounce off the metal interior of the oven because microwaves cannot pass through metal.

All foods prepared in the microwave cook from the outside toward the center. Microwaves strike the food from the exterior and penetrate 1 to 1½ inches. Small amounts of food arranged to a depth of not greater than 1½ inches heat more quickly than a casserole or whole chicken, for example, because the microwaves can penetrate all the way through. Larger items cook more slowly since the thickness beyond 1½ inches cooks by conduction, and it takes longer for the heat to reach the center of the food.

Installing Your Oven

Countertop microwave ovens plug into a standard grounded (three-prong) electric outlet. The ovens require 13 to 14 amps to operate and should be on a household circuit not supporting any other large user of electricity. A clock, lamp, or small kitchen appliance will not interfere with the microwave oven operation, but a microwave and a refrigerator on the same line will usually trip the circuit breaker if both are running at the same time.

Microwave ovens manufactured as part of a conventional oven arrangement should be installed according to the manufacturer's instructions.

Cooking Wattage

No electrical appliance is 100 percent efficient; it uses only a portion of its wattage. The portion of the wattage of a microwave that does the cooking is called the cooking wattage. Of all the facts you know about microwave cooking, this is one of the most important, because the cooking wattage determines how fast a microwave oven cooks. With this information you can select the correct cooking times from microwave recipes and more easily adapt conventional recipes to microwave cooking. Most microwave ovens range between 450 and 700 watts of cooking power. The 600- to 700-watt range is the most popular. The majority of recipes are written for ovens of these higher cooking powers and give a range of cooking times to accommodate this wattage range.

The recipes in this book are timed for 600- to 700-watt ovens. Use the shorter cooking time for the higher cooking wattage. (Check your use and care booklet for the additional time required.) When you try a new recipe, it's always wise to write down the actual time you used. This will eliminate guesswork each time you prepare the same food.

How do you find out cooking wattage information for your oven? Sometimes it's readily available but other times you must do some sleuthing. Begin with the use and care booklet or recipe book that accompanies your oven. Manufacturers usually include the information in the text or in a chart. If you recently purchased your oven, ask the salesperson. Or contact the manufacturer or the local service facility. Know the model number of your oven since each manufacturer has ovens of various wattages. Once you learn the cooking wattage, memorize it.

TIMING A MICROWAVE MEAL

Do you remember, when you were learning to cook, struggling to have all the foods for a meal ready to serve at the same time? Eventually, through practice, you became proficient and didn't have to plan as painstakingly.

Using your microwave to prepare whole meals will probably bring back memories of your early struggles. You are cooking the same foods, but suddenly they have different cooking times. In addition, you are preparing only one dish at a time. Don't panic. It's not as difficult as you think.

Consider the simple dinner shown above of Family Favorite Meat Loaf (see page 76), baked potatoes (see page 47), and steamed broccoli (see page 45) that you might fix to serve four people.

Cooking conventionally, you would start dinner by putting the meat loaf and potatoes in the oven. While they are baking, the broccoli could be steaming. Dinner would be hot and ready to serve about one hour after you began.

Now consider preparing the same meal in the microwave. Read the section on Standing Time, page 11. Then look at the directions for each food, noting how long it must cook and how long it needs to stand: meat loaf, cook 10 to 12 minutes, stand 10 minutes; baked potatoes, cook 12 to 14 minutes, stand 10 to 15 minutes; steamed broccoli, cook 5 to 7 minutes, stand 5 minutes. (As with conventional cooking you will soon memorize this information and will not have to look it up each time.)

The food with the longest cooking time will be cooked first. You'll cook the next dish while the previous dish is standing. Remember that the longer a food cooks, the longer it can stand without cooling off.

The correct microwave cooking order is: baked potatoes, 12 to 14 minutes; meat loaf, 10 to 12 minutes (meat loaf cooks during the 10 to 15 minutes the potatoes stand); steamed broccoli, 5 to 7 minutes (broccoli steams during the 10 minutes the meat loaf stands). Each item should be covered with aluminum foil during the standing time, so if the food must stand a few minutes longer than the recommended standing time, it will still be hot. This meal will be ready to serve in about 30 minutes.

This method works with any microwave menu. If something delays the serving time, use the microwave to quickly reheat the dishes. Because you will be busy preparing the meal, set the table before you start cooking.

You will not always prepare entire meals in the microwave. As you become proficient in its use, you will learn to combine cooking methods to make meal preparation quick and convenient.

BASIC MICROWAVE COOKWARE

Microwave cookware is available in an array of sizes, shapes, and materials; a list of the common types and sizes follows. Some dishes are labeled microwave-safe and others may need to be tested (see Is My Dish Microwave Safe?, page 12). Browning trays and dishes are made specifically for the microwave; for tips on how to use them, see Using a Browning Tray and Dish, page 13.

Cookware	Size	Material	Use
Covered casseroles	1 qt	Glass or plastic	Vegetables, desserts, casseroles, meats, soups
	1½ qt		
	2 qt		
	4 qt		
Round cake dish	8- or 9-in. diameter	Glass or plastic	Cakes, meat loaf
Square cake dish	8 or 9 in.	Glass or plastic	Bar cookies, seafood
Rectanglar baking dish	8 x 12 in.	Glass	Roasts, poultry, lasagne
Measuring cups	1 cup	Glass or plastic	Sauces, gravies, puddings, soups, drinks, melting butter
	2 cup		
	4 cup		
	8 cup		
Custard cups	6 oz	Glass	Eggs, custards
Pie plate	9-in. diameter	Glass	Pies, quiches, appetizers
Bundt dish	12-in. diameter	Plastic	Cakes
Ring dish	6 cup	Plastic	Cakes, breads, meat loaf
Muffin pan	Round, 6 cup	Plastic	Muffins, cupcakes
Tray	12-in. diameter	Glass	Appetizers, vegetables, cookies
Coffee or teapot	4 to 6 cup	Glass or plastic	Coffee and tea
Browning tray and dish	10 or 12 in.	Glass or plastic	Browning steaks, burgers, or chops
Meat rack	6 to 10 in.	Glass or plastic	Roasts, bacon
Thermometer		Glass or plastic	Roasting meats

Microwave Oven Features

Become familiar with all the features of your oven. You will use some more often than others, but all will be useful at times.

Controls There are two basic types of microwave oven controls—electronic and mechanical. By far the most popular are electronic controls since they operate easily by touch and can be programmed to do several steps in succession. Electronic controls also can be set for cooking powers and specific minutes and seconds.

Mechanical controls more closely resemble in appearance and operation the familiar controls on a conventional oven. A dial is turned to set the cooking time and power level.

A clock/timer may be part of the control on your oven or may be a separate indicator. Regardless of how the oven is designed, the controls are used to set the clock/timer, which allows the oven to cook for a specific amount of time, then to stop or shut off automatically.

Size Microwave ovens are available in a variety of sizes measured in overall exterior dimensions of the case and in the cubic-foot capacity of the interior. Your first consideration should be choosing an oven that will fit in the designated space in your kitchen. Once that requirement is met, choose an interior size to meet your needs.

Compared to conventional ovens, all microwave oven interiors appear small. Remember, however, that microwave cooking does not require hot air surrounding the food as does conventional cooking, so the food may more nearly fill the oven cavity. At least 1 inch of space is needed between the food and the oven wall so microwaves can bounce around. However, consider also that microwave ovens with smaller interiors can have lower cooking wattages.

Variable Powers The first microwave ovens had two power levels— on and off. It soon became apparent that other energy levels would allow

more choices for successful cooking. A defrost level was the first to be added so food could be defrosted without being cooked. The addition of other power levels has greatly expanded the variety of foods that can be microwaved with good results. Learning when to use these power levels is vital to successful microwave cooking.

Power levels are currently expressed in two ways: in terms such as high, medium, or low and in percentages of total power. These two methods are related since each refers to a percentage of power: high (100 percent), medium-high (90, 80, or 70 percent), medium (60 or 50 percent), medium-low (40, 30, or 20 percent), low (10 percent), and defrost (30 percent). Remember that the levels are percentages of the total cooking power and will vary from model to model. Always check the manufacturer's instructions for the proper equivalencies for your model oven. On some ovens the terms are printed on the controls. Other ovens can be programmed to cook at a

STANDARD ITEMS ADAPTABLE TO MICROWAVE USE

Many standard kitchen items can be used in the microwave.

Material	Use
Paper	
Towels and napkins	Short-term cooking and heating. Prolonged use can cause paper to scorch or burn. Avoid recycled paper, which may contain bits of metal.
Waxed paper	A light cover that holds in some steam. Does not stick to foods.
Plastic	
Styrofoam cups and plates	Short-term heating. Foods with high fat content will cause distortion or melting.
Plastic wrap	Forms tight cover to hold in steam. Vent by turning back corner to prevent splitting.
Cooking bags, boil-in bags*	Forms tight cover to hold in steam. Avoid using metal ties; close with plastic or fabric ties. Pierce with knife tip to prevent steam buildup.
Plastic storage containers	May be used for defrosting foods with low fat or sugar content. High heat will distort or damage plastic.
Special microwave plastics	Designed for microwave oven use. Follow manufacturer's instructions. Some are safe in conventional ovens also.
Glass and ceramic	
Oven cookware	Many brand names available. Attractive and safe for cooking, serving, and storing. Do not use plastic storage lids in microwave.
Dinnerware	Check for microwave-safe label or test it yourself. Do not use dishes with metal trim.
Wood and wicker	
Baskets, spoons, skewers, boards	Safe for short-term heating. Continued exposure to microwaves will remove natural moisture, causing splitting.
Metal	
Aluminum foil, shallow frozen-dinner trays	Check use and care book for manufacturer's recommendation.
Pots, pans, trays, spoons	Do not use.

*Ready-to-heat frozen foods are often packaged in boil-in bags.

percentage of the total power. The recipes in this book give both the terms and percentages to assist you.

Turntables Some microwave ovens have a built-in turntable in the cooking chamber. The turntable is designed to rotate the food for more even exposure to microwave energy; it eliminates the necessity of manually rotating the food to achieve even cooking (see Special Microwave Techniques, page 10). The recipes in this book allow you to decide when to rotate the food, depending on the oven model you have. Turntables are available as separate accessories to be used in microwave ovens without a built-in turntable. Before you decide to purchase this accessory, use your oven to cook a variety of foods. You may be pleased with the results without a turntable.

If a turntable is part of your oven design, always leave it in place when operating the microwave oven. Removing it usually produces very uneven cooking.

Conditions Affecting Microwave Cooking Results

Conditions that may influence the results of microwave cooking include the moisture content of the food, sugar and fat content, quantity, size and shape, temperature, density, and texture. Understanding each variable is essential to successful microwave cooking.

Moisture Content of Food Because microwave ovens cook by heating water molecules, food with a high moisture content cooks faster. Items with no moisture usually do not become warm, which explains why paper and glass are not heated by microwaves.

Sugar and Fat Content of Food Food with a high sugar and fat content cooks quickly since these ingredients heat rapidly in a microwave. Sugar and fat also enhance microwave browning and crisping, as evidenced by cooking bacon in the microwave.

Quantity of Food The more food you put in a microwave oven, the longer it takes to cook. For example, the time required to bake one potato is considerably less than the time needed to bake four potatoes.

9

Size and Shape of Food The size and shape of a food will help to determine the speed at which it cooks. Larger food items such as a roast or turkey require longer cooking times simply because they are larger masses of food and it takes longer for the heat to reach the center. The smaller size of peas and broccoli florets, for example, allow microwaves to penetrate more quickly for faster cooking.

Rounded food shapes cook evenly since microwaves can penetrate uniformly on all sides. Elongated food shapes with thick and thin areas are more likely to cook unevenly. Shielding these foods and rotating them assists even cooking (see Rotating and Shielding below).

Density and Texture of Food
Porous foods cook faster than dense foods since microwaves penetrate them more easily. Some foods, such as broccoli, have both dense and porous textures; the stems are much more dense than the open texture of the florets. You can assist even microwave penetration of a food such as this by careful placement during cooking. Arrange the broccoli stalks in a circle with the stems pointing toward the outside and the florets toward the center. The microwaves penetrate the stems first and start to cook them before reaching the florets. The result will be evenly cooked broccoli (see photograph below).

Temperature of Food Refrigerated foods require a longer cooking time than room-temperature foods because the microwaves must first heat the food to overcome the refrigerated temperature and then heat the food until it is hot and cooked.

10

Special Microwave Techniques

Microwave cooking requires learning some new techniques. You will recognize some of these as conventional techniques used in different ways.

Rotating Rotating involves turning around the container of food in the microwave during cooking. Since later-model microwave ovens are designed to cook more evenly than early-model ovens, frequent rotating may be unnecessary in newer ovens. Ovens with turntables do the rotating for you (see Turntables, page 9).

Watch the food in your oven carefully to determine how evenly it is cooking. If the food in one area of an oven always begins to cook sooner, your oven has a hot spot. Rotating the food will prevent overcooking in that spot. Establish a pattern of always rotating in the same direction (either clockwise or counterclockwise) to be sure the food is evenly cooked (see photograph below).

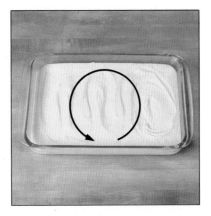

Turning This technique differs from rotating because it involves turning the food over rather than rotating the dish. Using a fork or tongs, turn the food upside down to allow microwaves to penetrate all sides. You may need to do this when baking large potatoes or cooking chicken parts.

Stirring You have been using this technique since you learned to cook. However, in microwave preparation stirring is done during the cooking time. This redistributes the food in the dish, exposing all parts evenly to microwave penetration.

Arranging Always try to place pieces of food in a circular pattern in the microwave. Place smaller, thinner, less fleshy foods toward the center of the dish or oven. Leave thicker, larger foods around the outside so all the foods receive adequate microwave penetration. These suggestions, however, may not always hold true; you may find that different-sized pieces of food or oven hot spots require you to rearrange the food at least once during cooking.

Covering Of all the microwave cooking techniques, this one probably creates the most uncertainty for cooks. It's an old technique that we have all used; yet knowing when to cover and with what seems confusing in microwave cooking. Here's a simple rule that works well and is easy to remember: If you want the food to be steamed during cooking, cover; if steam is unnecessary, cover only to cut down on spattering.

Foods you would cook covered conventionally usually should be covered in the microwave, such as steamed vegetables. Foods that are not covered conventionally are frequently not covered in the microwave, such as cakes and bar cookies.

To cover tightly, use plastic wrap (leave one corner open slightly) or a well-fitting lid; both hold in steam. To prevent spattering, use paper towels, napkins, or waxed paper (they do not fit tightly enough to steam the food). Paper towels and napkins have the advantage of being absorbent.

Shielding Use strips of aluminum foil to stop the microwaves from cooking selected areas of food (see photograph below). Because microwaves cannot pass through metal,

aluminum foil can prevent over-cooked corners of foods such as bar cookies or thin, bony areas on chicken or turkey wings or drumstick tips. Follow the manufacturer's directions for your oven in order to determine how much foil can be used in it. Be sure the aluminum foil does not touch the sides of the oven; if it does, arcing may occur, which could damage the oven.

Standing Time Although there are no microwaves present if the oven is not operating, all microwaved foods continue to cook after the oven shuts off because of the heat in the food. The amount of time the food continues to cook is called the standing time; when called for in a microwave recipe, it is necessary to allow for it. Serving food directly from the oven without letting it stand for the prescribed standing time may result in undercooked food.

Standing time ranges from 1 to 15 minutes. Generally, foods can stand the same amount of time they are cooked (up to 15 minutes) unless the recipe specifies a standing time. Standing 15 minutes is sufficient even for food cooked longer than that. If food continues to stand much beyond 15 minutes, it cools off and may need to be reheated. Standing time can occur in the microwave or on the countertop. Food that is meant to be served hot usually should be covered during standing to retain heat; the most effective cover is aluminum foil or a lid.

Many foods have the same indications of doneness whether they are cooked in a microwave or a conventional oven. The recipes in this book give you specific signs to look for when checking to see if the food is cooked. Experience will be a great help in making this judgment, so always observe carefully the appearance of the cooked food.

DEFROSTING FOODS IN THE MICROWAVE

Most microwave ovens have a special defrost setting, which is usually about 30 percent of the total cooking wattage. This setting allows the ice

DEFROSTING GUIDE FOR FROZEN FOODS

If your oven does not have a defrost setting, defrost on 30% power. Vegetables can be cooked frozen; defrosting is not necessary.

Food	Timing
Meats	
Roasts	5 to 6 min/lb
Steaks and chops	6 to 7 min/lb
Ground meats	5 to 7 min/lb
Poultry	
Whole bird	4 to 7 min/lb
Parts	4 to 5½ min/lb
Fish (watch carefully and stop if fish begins to cook)	
Whole fish or fillets	3 to 4½ min/lb
Shrimp, lobster tails, crabmeat	3 to 4 min/lb
Casseroles (break up and stir as soon as	
defrosting begins)	3 to 5 min/cup
Breads and cakes	1 to 3 min/serving

crystals in frozen food to melt without the food being cooked. Some microwave oven manufacturers automatically program the defrost cycle to turn on and off, allowing temperatures to equalize and preventing foods from starting to cook.

Frozen foods should be lightly covered during defrosting to prevent moisture loss. You may use freezer paper, waxed paper, or a plastic bag left open.

The chart above provides some general defrost timings. Your microwave oven use and care book will provide additional help.

IT'S A MICROWAVE FACT

☐ Microwave ovens use less energy than do conventional ovens and stovetops.

☐ Microwave ovens are safe when used as directed. The radiation produced by a microwave oven is non-ionizing radiation, which, unlike X rays or solar rays, cannot be stored in body tissue. And ovens are designed to prevent microwaves from escaping during use.

☐ Food cooked in a microwave oven can have fewer calories than the same dish prepared convention-

ally, because microwave preparation calls for a minimum of butter or margarine to grease pans, cook vegetables, and baste poultry. In addition, food cooked in a microwave oven has a fresh flavor that helps eliminate the need for rich sauces or gravies.

☐ Food prepared in a microwave oven contains more nutrients than the same food prepared conventionally. Studies conducted at Cornell University show that water-soluble vitamins are retained in food prepared properly in the microwave because less liquid is required for cooking.

☐ Contrary to popular belief, some microwave-safe dishes become hot during microwave cooking because they absorb heat from the hot food. This is especially true of food that is cooked tightly covered. Keep pot holders handy. (To determine if a dish is microwave-safe, see Is My Dish Microwave Safe?, page 12.)

☐ Food can burn in a microwave oven, although not as readily as on a stovetop or in a conventional oven. If food is cooked too long in the microwave, it will appear, taste, and smell burned. Proper timing is important.

REHEATING GUIDE

The times for these commonly reheated foods will serve as a quick reference. Use the high (100%) power setting; if the food begins to cook, reduce the power level to medium (50%) and add time.

Food	Container	Time
Vegetables	Covered casserole or dish	30 to 60 sec/cup. Stir once.
Casseroles	Covered casserole or dish	1½ to 2 min/cup. Stir once.
Meats and poultry (gravy or small amount of liquid will prevent overheating)	Plate or shallow baking dish, covered	30 to 45 sec/serving
Fish	Covered casserole or plate	20 to 40 sec/serving
Rice or pasta	Covered casserole or dish	1 to 2 min/cup. Stir once.
Bread, rolls, muffins, coffee cakes	Wrap in paper towel or napkin	10 to 15 sec/serving
Pie, cobbler, cake	Serving plate	10 to 20 sec/serving
Complete meal	Covered serving plate (all foods of similar thickness)	If food has been refrigerated, 1½ to 2½ min; if at room temperature, 1 to 2 min. Stir if possible.

REHEATING FOODS IN THE MICROWAVE

The microwave is a star when you want to reheat foods. The just-cooked flavors make leftovers a treat and nutritious snacks possible for even children to prepare. If your oven has a reheat setting, follow the manufacturer's suggestions for reheating foods. Because foods reheat best when covered, cover tightly if steaming or lightly if warming. You will quickly learn that when you can smell the food, it has usually reached serving temperature.

IS MY DISH MICROWAVE SAFE?

If you're in doubt about using a specific item in the microwave, here's how to test it for microwave safety.

1. Place a glass measure filled to the 1-cup mark with tap water in the microwave oven.

2. Place empty item you are testing in the microwave oven. Do not put water in item being tested since heat may transfer from water to item, giving a false indication of microwave safety of item.

3. Operate microwave on high (100%) 1 minute.

4. If the water is warm or hot and item has not heated, the item is safe to use in the microwave.

5. If the water is warm but item is hot, the item has absorbed microwave energy, making it unsafe for more extended microwave use because it may break. (Breakage should not occur during this test.)

CONVERTING CONVENTIONAL RECIPES

☐ Convert a recipe you are familiar with; if using an unfamiliar recipe, prepare it conventionally at least once before trying the conversion. You need to know how the completed food should look and taste.

☐ Remember that microwaves heat water molecules, so moist foods will convert most easily to microwave cooking. Look for recipes that have liquid in the ingredients. Those that are steamed or boiled and require covering are good candidates.

☐ The following foods are best prepared conventionally: broiled foods, deep-fried foods, hard-cooked eggs, and angel food cakes or puff pastries.

☐ Check a microwave cookbook for a similar recipe when converting a conventional dish. This will give you an indication of the power level for cooking as well as the time needed and any special instructions for turning or stirring.

☐ Recipes that can be stirred adapt well to microwave cooking. If the recipe calls for layering, and stirring will disturb the layers, it is difficult to heat the food evenly. Using a low-power setting can be substituted for stirring.

☐ Note the size of the dish required; make sure it will fit in your microwave. If it does not, perhaps the recipe could be divided and cooked in two dishes. One dish could be frozen and reheated for another time.

☐ For greater success in some recipes, prepared foods or quick-cooking foods can substitute for certain ingredients. For example, processed cheeses melt more evenly than hard or dry cheeses, and quick-cooking rice cooks in the same amount of time as other ingredients in a casserole (whereas conventional rice may require precooking).

☐ Always note substitutions of conventional recipe ingredients and successful timings you used.

CARING FOR YOUR MICROWAVE

☐ Cook fatty foods covered with a lid or paper towel to cut down on spattering inside oven.

☐ Remove grime and spatters as soon as possible; do not allow them to build up. To remove food spatters stuck to interior surfaces, place 1 cup water in the oven and microwave on high (100%) until water boils rapidly. Allow boiled water to stand in closed oven at least 5 minutes. Steam will loosen food particles. Then wipe oven interior with clean, damp cloth and mild dishwashing soap or detergent. The glass tray found on the bottom of some microwave ovens may be removed for easier washing.

☐ Wipe door seal with warm, soapy water and keep seal free of all grime buildup so door will close securely.

☐ Wipe exterior surfaces of oven with damp cloth and mild dish-washing soap or detergent.

☐ Touch-control panels may be wiped with damp cloth and polished lightly with dry dish towel.

☐ Keep paper and utensils away from exterior vents so air will circulate properly through oven.

☐ To remove occasional lingering food odors, place 1 tablespoon lemon juice in 1 cup water in the oven and microwave on high (100%) until water boils rapidly. Allow boiled mixture to stand in oven at least 5 minutes.

Step·by·Step

USING A BROWNING TRAY AND DISH

These utensils are designed to be preheated in the microwave oven before food is cooked on them; they brown food because they are hot when the food is placed on them. Designed specifically for microwave ovens, the utensils should not be used for conventional cooking. Browning utensils are available as dishes with sides and a lid and as trays or grills, which are flat and may have a well to collect drippings. The choice between a dish and a tray or grill should be determined by the food you want to cook. Some stir-frying techniques require a browning dish because it has sides; for cooking only burgers or steaks, the flat tray or grill with a well for drippings may be your best choice.

Browning utensils have a metal coating on the bottom that absorbs microwave energy during preheating, becoming very hot. Be careful never to touch the hot bottom with your fingertips.

Several recipes in this book specify browning utensils. Here are some tips on how to use them:

2. *Without removing hot utensil from oven, add food to be cooked. Do not overcrowd. Food will sizzle on hot surface. Microwave on high (100%) following recipe directions until bottom surface of food is browned. Food will partially cook.*

1. *Place empty browning utensil in microwave oven. Preheat utensil by microwaving on high (100%) following recipe directions. If desired, add butter or oil during the last minute of preheating time.*

3. *With spatula turn food over. Microwave according to recipe directions to brown second side and finish cooking food. (If item is large you may want to preheat utensil again for 1 or 2 minutes before browning second side.) Grease spatters during microwave browning just as it does in conventional browning, so wipe out oven after using with a damp cloth and mild dishwashing soap.*

Baked Stuffed Clams (see page 16), an herbed mixture of clams, onion, garlic, and bread crumbs served in the shells, is an easy and appealing first course.

Beginnings With Style

Innovative appetizers set the tone for
what's to come. Make elegant Two-Pepper
Appetizer Cheesecake (see page 16) the star
of the appetizer spread at an open house.
For both fast and fancy affairs, consider Quick
Appetizers (see page 20), which emphasize
simple preparation and readily available
ingredients. Complete the presentation with hot
Mulled Wine (see page 30), a cooling
Strawberry Shrub (see page 29), or delicious
Irish Coffee (see page 28). This chapter
also has suggestions for tasty breakfasts, from
a zesty Spanish Omelet (see page 35)
and fruity Pear Coffee Cake (see page 31) to
a scrambled egg for one prepared in
1 minute—all cooked in a microwave oven.

APPETIZERS

Fast and simple to prepare and festive to eat, appetizers are the fun part of a meal. Microwave ovens make appetizer preparation even quicker, and spending less time in the kitchen and more time with guests is a goal for every cook. The following microwave recipes should help you prepare delicious appetizers in a flash. When you serve more than one appetizer in a cocktail spread, you cannot be certain how frequently your guests will return for more. These appetizers will be popular, so plan to make extra.

CHEDDAR-SAUSAGE QUICHE

Cooking the quiche on the medium power setting (50%) allows the egg and cheese mixture to set without being overcooked.

- 1 unbaked pie shell (9 in.)
- ½ pound pork sausage
- 4 eggs, slightly beaten
- ¼ teaspoon salt
- ¼ teaspoon freshly ground pepper
- ¼ teaspoon ground sage
- ½ cup milk
- 1 cup grated Cheddar cheese Paprika, for sprinkling

1. Place pie shell in a microwave-safe pie plate; prick bottom and sides of shell with fork. Microwave on high (100%) until shell begins to appear dry in some areas (3 to 4 minutes). Let cool.

2. In a 2-quart microwave-safe bowl, crumble sausage. Microwave on high until sausage is lightly browned (4 to 5 minutes), stirring twice to break up sausage. Drain.

3. To drained sausage add eggs, salt, pepper, sage, and milk; mix well.

4. Sprinkle cheese in bottom of cooled pie shell. Pour sausage mixture over cheese and sprinkle with paprika. Microwave on medium (50%) until quiche is set (9 to 11 minutes). Let stand 10 minutes.

Serves 6.

TWO-PEPPER APPETIZER CHEESECAKE

Make this savory cheesecake a day before you want to serve it. Then chill it in the refrigerator until it is firm (at least 8 hours). Serve this very rich dish in thin wedges.

- ¼ cup plus 1 tablespoon butter or margarine
- 1 cup rye cracker crumbs (about thirty-two 2-inch crackers)
- 1 large green bell pepper, chopped
- 1 large red bell pepper, chopped
- 1 medium onion, chopped
- 2 packages (8 oz each) cream cheese
- 4 eggs
- ¼ cup milk

1. In a 9-inch-diameter microwave-safe baking dish or microwave springform pan, microwave ¼ cup of the butter on high (100%) until melted (30 to 60 seconds). Stir in cracker crumbs; press mixture firmly in bottom of dish. Set aside.

2. In a 1-quart microwave-safe casserole, combine the remaining 1 tablespoon butter, green and red pepper, and onion. Cover and microwave on high until pepper and onion are crisp-tender (2 to 4 minutes), stirring once. Set aside.

3. In a medium microwave-safe mixing bowl, place cream cheese. Microwave on medium (50%) until softened (2 to 3 minutes). Add eggs and milk and beat until well mixed. Fold in cooked vegetables. Microwave on high until hot (4 to 6 minutes), stirring twice.

4. Pour mixture over cracker crumbs in baking dish. Microwave on medium until cheese mixture appears almost set (7 to 10 minutes). Let cool; then refrigerate 8 hours or overnight. Cheesecake will firm as it chills.

Makes one 9-inch cheesecake.

BAKED STUFFED CLAMS

Serve these stuffed clams in their shells as a delectable first course.

- 1 tablespoon olive oil
- 1 tablespoon chopped onion
- 2 cloves garlic, minced
- 10 to 12 fresh clams, washed, shucked, and minced or 1 can (10 oz) minced clams, liquid reserved
- 1 tablespoon chopped parsley
- ½ teaspoon dried oregano
- ½ cup fine, dried bread crumbs
- 12 clamshells, to fill Paprika, for sprinkling Lemon wedges, for garnish

1. In a 2-quart microwave-safe casserole, combine oil, onion, and garlic. Microwave on high (100%) until onion is soft (1 to 2 minutes). Stir in clams and microwave on high until clams are opaque (1 to 2 minutes). Add parsley, oregano, and bread crumbs, stirring until well mixed. If very dry add 1 to 3 teaspoons reserved clam liquid.

2. Into each of 12 clamshells spoon 1 heaping tablespoon clam mixture. On a microwave-safe plate arrange stuffed shells in a circular pattern. Microwave on high until clam mixture is hot (2 to 3 minutes). Sprinkle with paprika and serve with lemon.

Makes 12 shells.

CHICKEN AND BROCCOLI QUICHE

Cut this quiche into narrow wedges and top each with a thin strip of sweet red pepper for a bright spot on your appetizer table.

- 1 unbaked pie shell (9 in.)
- 1 whole chicken breast
- 4 eggs, slightly beaten
- ¼ teaspoon salt
- ¼ teaspoon freshly ground pepper
- 1 cup milk
- 1½ cups chopped broccoli, cooked
- 1 cup grated Swiss cheese Sliced red bell pepper, for garnish (optional)

1. Place pie shell in a microwave-safe pie plate; prick bottom and sides of shell with fork. Microwave on high (100%) until shell begins to look dry in some areas (3 to 4 minutes). Let cool.

2. Place chicken breast on a microwave-safe plate. Cover with waxed paper and microwave on high until chicken is tender and juices are clear when chicken is pierced with a fork (2 to 3 minutes). Let cool; cut into ½-inch cubes.

3. In a large bowl combine chicken cubes, eggs, salt, pepper, milk, broccoli, and cheese. Pour mixture into cooled pie shell. Microwave on medium (50%) until quiche is set (9 to 11 minutes). Let stand 10 minutes. Cut into wedges and garnish with red bell pepper, if desired.

Serves 6.

COLOMBIAN SUGARED PEANUTS

This appetizer from Colombia, South America, quickly converted to an easy microwave version. Eat these peanuts at once or store them tightly covered.

> ¾ cup sugar
> 3 tablespoons water
> 2 cups roasted unsalted peanuts

1. In a 1½-quart microwave-safe casserole, combine all ingredients. Microwave on high (100%) until mixture boils (5 to 7 minutes), stirring twice.

2. Remove peanuts with slotted spoon and spread in single layer on a glass tray. Microwave on high until peanuts are toasted and dry (4 to 6 minutes). Do not burn.

3. Turn out on waxed paper, breaking peanuts apart. Let cool.

Makes 2 cups.

Two-Pepper Appetizer Cheesecake, made of smooth cream cheese studded with chopped bell pepper and baked in a crispy rye-crumb crust, is a marvelous surprise for a first course. Garnish it with cream-cheese rosettes and slivers of red and green bell pepper.

Glistening shrimp and slivers of lemon zest and bell pepper are banded with bacon slices in these tasty Shrimp Wrap-Ups. Assemble them ahead of time; they will keep well in the refrigerator for up to 8 hours.

2. Cover evenly with mayonnaise. Sprinkle with cheese.

3. Microwave on medium (50%) until hot and bubbly and cheese is melted (3 to 5 minutes). Serve immediately with corn chips.

Makes about 2 cups.

SHRIMP WRAP-UPS

Multiply this recipe for a large party and keep the wrap-ups coming hot from the microwave, but for best results cook no more than 16 (one recipe) at a time.

    8 slices bacon
   16 large raw shrimp, peeled and
       deveined, tails on
       Zest of 1 lemon, slivered
    1 green bell pepper, slivered
    2 tablespoons soy sauce
    2 tablespoons dry white wine
    2 tablespoons chili sauce
    2 tablespoons plum or
       grape jelly

1. Arrange 4 slices bacon on paper towel and cover with another paper towel. Arrange remaining 4 slices bacon on top and cover with another paper towel. Microwave on high (100%) until bacon is slightly browned but not fully cooked (4 minutes).

2. Cut bacon slices in half. Wrap each piece of bacon around 1 shrimp, 1 sliver zest, and 1 sliver pepper. Secure each wrap-up with toothpick. Arrange wrap-ups in an 8-inch microwave-safe baking dish.

3. In a 2-cup microwave-safe measure, mix soy sauce, wine, chili sauce, and jelly. Pour over wrap-ups.

4. Microwave on high until shrimp are pink (3 to 4 minutes).

Makes 16.

<u>Note</u> To assemble wrap-ups ahead of time, complete recipe through step 3, cover, and refrigerate. Then heat and serve.

HOT ARTICHOKE CHEESE DIP

Cooking this dip on medium power allows it to heat completely without being stirred, preserving the individual layers. If you are in a rush, mix all the ingredients together and microwave on high 1 to 2 minutes, stirring once.

    1 can (8 oz) artichoke hearts in
       water, drained
    1 jar (6 oz) marinated
       artichoke hearts, drained
    1 can (4 oz) green chiles,
       drained
    6 tablespoons mayonnaise
  1½ cups shredded Cheddar cheese
       Corn chips, for dipping

1. Chop all artichoke hearts. Distribute evenly in a 9-inch glass pie plate. Scatter chiles on top.

QUICK GARBANZO APPETIZER

Garbanzo beans are a nutritious, high-protein addition to any meal. Serve these versatile beans hot or chilled as a first course, as part of an antipasto platter, or added to tossed salad.

 1 tablespoon olive oil
 ½ teaspoon salt
 ¼ teaspoon pepper
 1 can (16 oz) garbanzo beans
   Lettuce leaves, for serving
 2 tablespoons chopped parsley,
   for garnish

1. In a 1-quart microwave-safe casserole, combine olive oil, salt, and pepper. Microwave on high (100%) until oil is heated (1 to 1½ minutes).

2. Drain beans and add to olive oil mixture. Microwave on high until hot (1½ to 2 minutes), stirring twice.

3. Mound bean mixture on lettuce-lined plate. Sprinkle with chopped parsley. Serve with individual plates and forks.

Makes 2 cups.

Note Beans may be prepared ahead and stored in the refrigerator; they will keep 3 to 4 days. Serve chilled or reheat in microwave on high until hot (1 to 1½ minutes).

HOT CRABMEAT SPREAD

Try substituting an equal amount of minced clams for the crabmeat for a variation of this spread.

 1 package (8 oz) cream cheese,
   softened
 1 tablespoon milk
 ¼ pound fresh crabmeat or
   1 can (7 oz) crabmeat,
   drained and flaked
 2 green onions, chopped
 ½ teaspoon prepared horseradish
 ¼ teaspoon freshly ground
   pepper
 2 tablespoons slivered almonds,
   for sprinkling
   Crackers, for accompaniment

1. In a medium bowl thoroughly combine cream cheese and milk. Add crabmeat, green onion, horseradish, and pepper. Mix well.

2. Turn crabmeat mixture into an 8-inch glass pie plate and smooth top. Sprinkle with almonds.

3. Microwave on medium-high (70%) until heated through (2 to 3 minutes). Serve immediately with crackers.

Makes about 2 cups.

CHINESE PORK BALLS

Dim sum means *heart's delight.* Traditionally a selection of sweet and savory foods served throughout the day, many dim sum dishes, such as pork balls, are excellent choices for Western appetizers.

 1 pound ground pork
 1 can (8 oz) water chestnuts,
   drained
 1 tablespoon finely chopped
   fresh ginger
 1 tablespoon soy sauce
 1 egg
 1 tablespoon vegetable oil
   Plum sauce or Chinese hot
   mustard, for dipping

1. In medium bowl combine pork, water chestnuts, ginger, soy sauce, and egg. Mix thoroughly and shape into 1-inch-diameter balls.

2. Preheat a microwave browning dish 3 minutes on high (100%). Add vegetable oil and microwave on high 1 minute.

3. Place as many meatballs in dish as will fit without crowding. Microwave on high 2 to 3 minutes, stirring to brown all sides. Transfer to serving plate and repeat with remaining meatballs. Serve immediately with plum sauce.

Makes 30 meatballs.

Note If meatballs are made ahead, reheat on a microwave-safe plate by microwaving on high until hot (1 to 3 minutes), stirring once.

... FOR APPETIZERS

These helpful suggestions will make microwave appetizers easy to prepare and serve.

☐ Cheeses can be softened in the microwave for easier mixing. Microwave on high (100%) 30 to 45 seconds. Remember to remove aluminum foil wrapping.

☐ Mix dips and spreads in microwave-safe serving dishes or bowls so they can be reheated easily.

☐ Use medium (50%) power setting when cooking cheese-based dips or spreads to prevent overcooking.

☐ Stir unlayered dips and spreads after microwaving to distribute heat evenly and eliminate any hot spots.

☐ Crisp stale crackers and chips by microwaving on high (100%) 30 to 45 seconds.

☐ Remember to select appetizers that will complement foods to follow.

☐ To plan quantities, count on each person at a cocktail party eating 2 to 3 servings of each food offered. At a dinner party, 6 to 8 servings is an average number per guest.

☐ Serve appetizers that do not all require last-minute microwaving. If they do, your speedy microwave will seem to tick off very slow seconds.

QUICK APPETIZERS

You can prepare a number of very simple appetizers quickly in the microwave with readily available ingredients. Once you try these, you are bound to come up with interesting combinations of your own. Some of the combinations are prepared to taste. Combine the ingredients as you like, heat in the microwave at the specified power setting, and serve warm.

Arrange the elements for these combinations in a circle on a microwave-safe plate:

☐ Top rich buttery crackers with shredded cheese of your choice. Microwave on high (100%) until cheese is melted.

☐ Top saltines with peanut butter and thinly sliced sweet onion or red onion. Microwave on high (100%) until warm.

☐ Top melba toast with tuna salad and slices of Swiss cheese. Microwave on medium-high (70%) until cheese is melted.

☐ Combine ground round and dry onion-mushroom soup mix, ½ box (2.5 oz total) soup mix to 1 pound meat, and shape into 1-inch-diameter balls. Microwave 8 to 10 meatballs at a time on high (100%) until browned. Serve on toothpicks.

Combine the ingredients for these appetizers in a microwave-safe bowl and microwave on high (100%):

☐ Combine taco sauce, chopped onion, and ground cumin. Spoon over tortilla chips. Sprinkle with shredded cheese and microwave until cheese is melted.

☐ Combine equal amounts of sharp cheese spread and minced clams. Microwave until cheese is melted. Season to taste with hot pepper sauce. Serve with crackers.

☐ Combine pineapple preserves and prepared mustard to taste, spoon over hot dog or Vienna sausage chunks, and microwave until sausage is hot. Stir to coat sausage with mustard mixture and serve with toothpicks.

☐ Add applesauce and ground cinnamon to precooked sausage chunks (½ teaspoon cinnamon and 1 cup applesauce to 12 ounces sausage links, cut up) and microwave until sausage is heated through, stirring once to coat sausage with applesauce mixture. Serve with toothpicks.

☐ Toss oyster crackers or small square cheese crackers with melted butter (1 tablespoon butter to 2 cups crackers) and microwave until crackers are warm. Sprinkle with Parmesan cheese, if desired, and serve in bowl.

A bit more preparation is required for this appetizer, but it is still quick:

☐ Slit 4-inch-long kielbasa sausage chunks partially through lengthwise and fill slits with pizza sauce and shredded mozzarella cheese. Skewer with toothpicks at 1-inch intervals, place on a microwave-safe plate, cover with waxed paper, and microwave on high (100%) until sausage is hot. Cut sausage between toothpicks and serve.

NUT-MUSHROOM SPREAD

This recipe is adapted from one written by Susan E. Mitchell that originally appeared in the California Culinary Academy series cookbook *30-Minute Meals.*

- 4 teaspoons butter
- 1 package (10 oz) whole blanched almonds
- 1 small onion
- 1 or 2 cloves garlic, peeled
- ¾ pound (30 medium) mushrooms
- ½ teaspoon salt
- ¼ teaspoon dried thyme
- ¼ cup unflavored yogurt or sour cream
- 1 to 2 tablespoons dry sherry, or to taste
  Crackers or sliced bread, for accompaniment

1. In a 1-quart microwave-safe casserole, microwave 1 teaspoon of the butter on high (100%) until melted (30 seconds). Add almonds and toss to coat. Microwave on high until toasted (2 to 3 minutes), stirring twice and watching carefully to avoid burning. Remove almonds from casserole and reserve.

2. Finely chop onion, garlic, and mushrooms. In the same casserole used to toast almonds, microwave the remaining 3 teaspoons butter on high until melted (30 to 60 seconds). Add chopped vegetables, salt, and thyme. Microwave on high until vegetables are soft (2 to 3 minutes).

3. Set aside ½ cup of the reserved almonds. In the work bowl of a food processor or blender, process remaining almonds until finely ground. Add cooked vegetables and yogurt and process until almost smooth. Add sherry and pulse to blend.

4. Place mixture in serving bowl, garnish with reserved almonds, cover, and refrigerate until chilled. Serve with crackers.

Makes about 3 cups.

FLUFFY EGG DIP

Serve this tangy egg dip with a tray of fresh vegetables or crisp crackers.

    2 eggs
    1 package (8 oz) cream cheese
    2 tablespoons milk
    2 tablespoons mayonnaise
    1 teaspoon prepared mustard
    ½ teaspoon ground cumin
    ¼ teaspoon salt
       Parsley, for garnish
       Assorted fresh vegetables
       or crisp crackers, for
       accompaniment

1. Grease a small microwave-safe casserole. Break one of the eggs into dish and puncture yolk with tines of a fork. Cover dish and microwave on high (100%) until yolk is solid (1 to 1½ minutes). Remove to bowl of food processor; repeat with second egg.

2. To cooked eggs in bowl of food processor, add cream cheese, milk, mayonnaise, mustard, cumin, and salt. Process until fluffy.

3. Transfer mixture to a small bowl. Garnish with parsley and serve with fresh vegetables.

Makes 1½ cups.

Mound this tangy egg dip in a colorful radicchio leaf and surround it with the freshest raw vegetables, including very thin asparagus spears, jicama sticks, baby carrots, slices of red and yellow bell pepper, and crisp zucchini rounds.

TACO DIP

Adjust the spiciness of this dip by choosing hot or mild taco sauce. The dip may be made ahead and reheated in the microwave until it is steaming (2 to 3 minutes on high). Add cheese just before serving.

- *1 pound ground beef*
- *1 medium onion, finely chopped*
- *1 can (6 oz) tomato paste*
- *1 jar (8 oz) taco sauce*
- *1 can (4 oz) green chiles, chopped*
- *2 tablespoons chili powder*
- *½ cup shredded sharp Cheddar cheese*
- *Tortilla chips, for accompaniment*

1. In a 2-quart microwave-safe dish, crumble ground beef. Microwave on high (100%) until meat is only slightly pink (2 to 3 minutes). Stir in onion and microwave on high until beef is browned and onion is soft (2 to 3 minutes). Drain.

2. Add tomato paste, taco sauce, chiles, and chili powder. Stir to combine. Cover and microwave on high 3 to 5 minutes, stirring twice.

3. Sprinkle with cheese and serve immediately with tortilla chips.

Makes 3 cups.

TUNA MOUSSE

A seafood mousse is a welcome addition to any cocktail party. This one can be made up to 48 hours ahead. Cover tightly and store in the refrigerator. To carry out the seafood theme, mold the mousse in a shell or fish shape.

- *½ cup cold water*
- *1 package unflavored gelatin*
- *2 cans (7 oz) water-packed tuna, drained and flaked*
- *2 cups mayonnaise*
- *½ cup seeded, chopped, and drained cucumber*
- *2 tablespoons grated onion*
- *½ teaspoon salt*
- *Lettuce leaves (optional)*
- *Cucumber slices (optional)*
- *Crackers, for accompaniment*

1. Place the water in a 1-cup microwave-safe measure. Sprinkle gelatin on the water. Microwave on high (100%) until gelatin is dissolved (30 seconds), stirring once. Set aside.

2. To work bowl of food processor or blender, add tuna, mayonnaise, cucumber, onion, and salt. Process until well mixed (5 to 10 seconds). Gradually add gelatin mixture and process until smooth.

3. Pour tuna mixture into oiled 6-cup mold. Chill until firm.

4. Unmold onto lettuce leaves and garnish with cucumber slices, if desired. Serve with crackers.

Makes 5 cups.

MUSHROOM-LIVER PÂTÉ

Prepare the pâté a day before you intend to use it and serve cold. It may be served directly from the mold or unmolded and served on a tray.

- *1 tablespoon vegetable oil*
- *1 tablespoon butter*
- *1 medium onion, chopped*
- *2 cloves garlic, minced*
- *½ pound chicken livers, rinsed and dried*
- *½ pound fresh mushrooms, sliced*
- *3 tablespoons minced parsley*
- *1 teaspoon salt*
- *¼ teaspoon freshly ground pepper*
- *1 tablespoon brandy*
- *Parsley or trumpet chanterelles, for garnish*
- *Crackers, for accompaniment*

1. In a 2-quart microwave-safe bowl, combine oil, butter, onion, and garlic. Microwave on high (100%) 3 to 4 minutes, stirring once.

2. Add chicken livers and mushrooms. Cover with paper towel. Microwave on medium (50%) until livers lose their pink color (4 to 6 minutes), stirring twice. Drain off and discard liquid.

3. Transfer mixture to work bowl of food processor or blender. Add minced parsley, salt, pepper, and brandy. Process until smooth. Pour into a 2-cup mold, cover, and chill at least 4 hours, or overnight.

4. Garnish with parsley and serve with crackers.

Makes 2 cups.

HOT BEEF DIP

Be prepared to pass along a copy of the recipe for this dip when you serve it at your next party. It is always a hit and makes plenty for a large crowd.

- *1 package (8 oz) cream cheese*
- *2 tablespoons milk*
- *1 tablespoon minced onion*
- *1 teaspoon garlic powder*
- *¼ teaspoon salt*
- *½ cup sour cream*
- *1 package (4 oz) dried or chipped beef*
- *1 tablespoon butter*
- *½ cup chopped pecans*
- *Crackers, for accompaniment*

1. In a 1-quart microwave-safe casserole, microwave cream cheese on high (100%) 30 to 60 seconds. Add milk, onion, garlic powder, salt, and sour cream. Cut dried beef into very fine slivers. Add to cream cheese mixture and mix well; smooth top.

2. In a small microwave-safe bowl, microwave butter on high until melted (30 to 60 seconds). Add pecans and stir to coat. Microwave on high until pecans are lightly toasted (2 to 3 minutes). Do not burn.

3. Sprinkle toasted pecans on top of cream cheese and beef mixture and microwave on medium-high (70%) until heated through but not bubbling (3 to 4 minutes). Serve with crackers.

Makes 1½ cups.

TURKEY PÂTÉ

This mild-flavored, low-fat pâté will be a favorite with dieters at your next cocktail party.

　1　tablespoon vegetable oil
　1½　pounds ground turkey
　½　cup each *finely chopped carrot, celery, and onion*
　2　*hard-cooked eggs, peeled and finely chopped*
　¼　cup dry white wine
　2　teaspoons dried dill
　1　teaspoon salt
　½　teaspoon freshly ground pepper
　　　Carrot curls, for garnish
　　　Assorted crackers, for accompaniment

1. Oil a 4-cup mold; set aside. In a 3-quart microwave-safe container, microwave oil on high (100%) 1 minute. Add turkey and chopped carrot, celery, and onion. Microwave on high until turkey is no longer pink and vegetables are tender (3 to 4 minutes), stirring once.

2. Add eggs, wine, dill, salt, and pepper. Transfer about one third of turkey mixture to work bowl of food processor and process until smooth. Remove processed mixture to oiled mold, packing mixture into mold and smoothing top. Repeat with remaining mixture.

3. Cover packed mold with plastic wrap and chill several hours or overnight. Unmold onto serving plate, garnish with carrot curls, and serve with assorted crackers.

Makes 3 cups.

Serve this smooth Mushroom-Liver Pâté on plain crackers so its subtle flavor will not be upstaged. Garnish with delicate trumpet chanterelles.

1. Unwrap Brie and place in a microwave-safe quiche dish or pie plate. Sprinkle with nuts. Cover top and sides with brown sugar, gently patting it in with your fingers. Do not be concerned if sides are not fully covered.

2. Microwave on medium-high (70%) until cheese is warm and soft (1 to 2 minutes), testing with a toothpick. Cheese should retain shape. Serve immediately with baguette slices.

Makes about 1 cup.

Note To reheat, return cheese to the microwave and microwave on medium (50%) until cheese is warm (30 to 60 seconds).

POPCORN TREAT

Flavored popcorn is a popular offering at some popcorn shops. Turn your microwave into a popcorn shop with this special treat. It is sure to be a hit with all ages.

> 1 package (3½ oz) salt-free microwave popcorn
> 1½ cups roasted salted peanuts
> 2 tablespoons butter
> 2 tablespoons honey
> ½ teaspoon ground cinnamon

1. Prepare popcorn according to package instructions. Place in bowl. Add peanuts and set aside.

2. In a 1-cup microwave-safe measure, combine butter, honey, and cinnamon. Microwave on high (100%) until butter is melted (30 to 60 seconds). Stir to combine.

3. Drizzle butter mixture over popcorn mixture. Toss to coat and serve immediately.

Makes 5 to 6 cups.

Note Popcorn can be reheated in the microwave on high until warm (1 to 2 minutes).

Crunchy nuts and glistening brown sugar top Sweet Brie, delicious served on baguette rounds and crisp apple slices.

SWEET BRIE

A tasty treat for Brie lovers, this appetizer can be prepared in a quiche dish and circled with baguette slices or crackers for easy serving.

> 1 wheel (4½ to 8 oz) Brie
> ½ cup chopped pecans or walnuts
> ¾ cup firmly packed brown sugar
> Sliced baguette or crackers, for accompaniment

FOOTBALL FARE

Hot Broccoli Dip

Assorted Crackers

French Bread Chunks

Cheese Football

Peanutty Party Mix

Hearty Bean Soup

Garlic-Stuffed Mushrooms

Cranberry Citrus Punch

Fresh Fruit

Chianti, Chenin Blanc, Beer

Invite friends to watch your favorite football team in action on a Sunday afternoon. This fine array of appetizers will make viewing the game more fun. The cheese dip molded in the shape of a football carries out the theme. The mushrooms, stuffed with garlic, pecans, and Parmesan, are irresistible. On a cold day the Hearty Bean Soup will be a welcome addition to this spread.

HOT BROCCOLI DIP

This pretty green dip looks appealing served in a microwave-safe red or yellow serving dish. If the dip cools before it is consumed, pop it back in the microwave and warm it on high (being sure to stir) until it is steaming again.

> 1 tablespoon butter or margarine
> 2 or 3 green onions, chopped
> 1 cup chopped celery
> 2 cloves garlic, minced
> 2 tablespoons flour
> 1 can (10½ oz) condensed cream of mushroom soup
> 1 cup grated Cheddar cheese
> 2 cups fresh broccoli florets, cooked, drained, and chopped or 1 package (10 oz) frozen chopped broccoli, cooked and drained (see Note)
> Crackers or French bread cut into chunks, for accompaniment

1. In a 3-quart microwave-safe casserole, microwave butter on high (100%) until melted (1 to 1½ minutes). Add green onion, celery, and garlic; microwave on high until vegetables are soft (4 to 5 minutes). Stir in flour.

2. Add soup and cheese and microwave on medium-high (70%) until soup is hot and cheese melts (3 to 4 minutes). Fold in cooked broccoli. Serve hot with crackers.

Makes 3 cups.

Note To cook frozen broccoli, place unopened package on microwave-safe dish and microwave on high (100%) until package is thawed (3 to 4 minutes).

CHEESE FOOTBALL

This large football-shaped cheese ball serves lots of fans for a Super Bowl or tailgate party. Be creative and mold the cheese into a firecracker shape for a Fourth of July party, adding streamers in patriotic colors. Or for the holidays mold the cheese into a pinecone shape and nestle it in greens on a serving platter.

> 2 packages (8 oz each) cream cheese
> 1 package (10 oz) sharp Cheddar cheese, shredded
> 1 package (10 oz) mild Cheddar cheese, shredded
> 2 teaspoons salt
> 1 tablespoon Worcestershire sauce
> 2 tablespoons grated onion
> 1 tablespoon minced parsley, plus parsley sprigs, for garnish
> Sliced almonds, for decorating
> Crackers, for accompaniment

1. In a large microwave-safe bowl, microwave cream cheese on medium (50%) 2 to 3 minutes. Stir until cream cheese is soft.

2. Add sharp and mild Cheddar to softened cream cheese. Microwave on medium 1 to 1½ minutes, then stir until cheese is soft.

3. Add salt, Worcestershire sauce, onion, and minced parsley, stirring to thoroughly blend seasonings into softened cheese mixture.

4. Form cheese mixture into football shape and place on a serving plate. Use sliced almonds to form football lacing pattern. Garnish plate with parsley sprigs. Cover and chill in refrigerator until firm. Serve at room temperature with crackers.

Makes 2 to 3 cups.

Pass the Cheese Football, Hot Broccoli Dip, and Garlic-Stuffed Mushrooms for a Sunday afternoon of watching football with friends.

PEANUTTY PARTY MIX

Party hash was a popular party snack for teenagers in the fifties. This microwave version can be prepared ahead (see Note). With its peanut butter coating, this would have been as big a hit then as it is today.

- 2 tablespoons butter or margarine
- 1/3 cup creamy peanut butter
- 2 cups bite-sized toasted wheat breakfast cereal
- 2 cups bite-sized toasted rice breakfast cereal
- 1 cup salted pretzel sticks or rings
- 1/2 cup roasted salted peanuts

1. In a large microwave-safe bowl, microwave butter on high (100%) until melted (30 to 60 seconds). Stir in peanut butter and microwave on high until warm (30 to 60 seconds). Stir until smooth.

2. Add cereals, pretzel sticks, and peanuts. Toss until coated with peanut butter mixture.

3. Microwave on high until warm and crispy (3 to 5 minutes). Serve immediately.

Makes 5 to 6 cups.

Note Party mix may be prepared ahead. Cover and store in refrigerator; reheat in the microwave on high until warm (1 to 3 minutes).

HEARTY BEAN SOUP

A blustery Sunday afternoon of watching football will be warmed by steaming mugs of this hearty soup.

- 1 pound dried Great Northern beans
- 8 cups hot water
- 2 medium carrots, cut in 1/4-inch dice
- 1 small onion, cut in 1/4-inch dice
- 1 cup diced ham (1/4-in. cubes)
- 1/2 teaspoon freshly ground pepper
- 3/4 teaspoon salt, or to taste
  Chopped parsley, for garnish (optional)

1. In a 4-quart microwave-safe casserole, place beans and the hot water. Cover and microwave on high (100%) until water is boiling (14 to 18 minutes). Stir.

2. Reduce power to medium (50%) and microwave, covered, until beans are nearly tender (50 to 60 minutes), stirring every 10 minutes.

3. Stir in carrots, onion, ham, and pepper. Microwave, covered, on high until vegetables are tender (8 to 10 minutes).

4. Remove 1 cup of the cooked beans and mash slightly with the back of a spoon; return mashed beans to soup. Season soup with salt. Let stand, covered, 10 minutes.

5. Ladle soup into mugs and garnish with chopped parsley, if desired.

Makes about 6 cups, serves 6.

GARLIC-STUFFED MUSHROOMS

Lovers of garlic may prefer a more garlicky flavor. Adjust the amount of garlic to suit your taste.

- 12 medium mushrooms
- 2 tablespoons butter
- 2 green onions, thinly sliced
- 2 cloves garlic, minced, or to taste
- 1 1/2 tablespoons ground pecans
- 1 1/2 tablespoons unflavored dried bread crumbs
- 1 1/2 tablespoons grated Parmesan cheese
- 1/2 teaspoon salt
- 1/4 teaspoon ground pepper
  Paprika, for sprinkling

1. Wipe mushrooms with a damp cloth to remove dirt; remove stems and reserve. Place mushroom caps on a microwave-safe plate lined with a paper towel, stem side down. Microwave on high (100%) until hot (2 to 2 1/2 minutes). Set aside.

2. Chop reserved stems. Place chopped stems, butter, green onion, and garlic in a 2-cup microwave-safe measure. Microwave on high until vegetables are soft (2 to 3 minutes), stirring once. Add pecans, bread crumbs, cheese, salt, and pepper; stir until well combined.

3. Stuff each mushroom cap with mixture. Place stuffed mushrooms on microwave-safe plate lined with a paper towel. Sprinkle with paprika. Microwave until heated through (2 to 3 minutes). Serve immediately.

Makes 12 mushrooms, serves 6.

CRANBERRY CITRUS PUNCH

Make this spicy punch ahead to serve a crowd. The brilliant color sparkles through a clear glass punch bowl.

- 1 bottle (48 oz) cranberry juice cocktail
- 1/4 cup sugar
- 6 whole cloves, stems attached
- 4 orange slices (1/4 in. thick each)
- 2 cinnamon sticks (3 in. each)
- 2 cups orange juice

Orange Juice Ring

- 1 medium orange, thinly sliced
- 2 cups orange juice

1. To a 4-quart microwave-safe dish, add 1 1/2 cups of the cranberry juice cocktail. Stir in sugar. Insert cloves into orange slices and float on top. Stir in cinnamon sticks. Microwave on high (100%) until punch is hot and sugar is dissolved (3 to 4 minutes), stirring twice.

2. Add remaining cranberry juice cocktail and orange juice. Refrigerate until chilled.

3. To serve, unmold Orange Juice Ring and place in punch bowl. Pour punch over ring.

Makes twenty 3-ounce servings.

Orange Juice Ring

1. Cut each orange slice in half crosswise and arrange halved slices in bottom of a 4-cup ring mold. Pour 1/2 cup of the juice on halved slices and place in freezer 1 hour.

2. Remove from freezer, add the remaining 1 1/2 cups juice, and place in freezer 8 hours or until solid.

BEVERAGES

Hot beverages are readily available with the microwave, but don't overlook the cool beverages you can prepare ahead and have chilling in the refrigerator. Some recipes are sized for parties; others are given in individual portions. Treat yourself or double the recipe and sip with a friend.

PEACH CAPPUCCINO

This delicious drink is the grand finale to a quiet dinner for two. Sip slowly and enjoy.

- ½ cup milk or half-and-half
- ¼ cup peach-flavored schnapps
- ½ cup hot espresso (see Note)
  Freshly ground nutmeg, for sprinkling

1. In a 2-cup microwave-safe measure, combine milk and schnapps. Microwave on medium (50%) until hot but not boiling (1 to 2 minutes).

2. Pour hot milk mixture and hot espresso into blender. Process 10 seconds. Divide between 2 espresso cups. Sprinkle with nutmeg and serve.

Serves 2.

Note To brew instant espresso microwave ½ cup water on high (100%) until boiling (1 to 1½ minutes). Stir in 1 teaspoon granulated instant espresso.

IRISH COFFEE

Make this fine after-dinner drink as an individual treat or double the recipe and share an Irish toast with a friend.

- 1½ cups water
- 3 teaspoons granulated instant coffee
- ½ teaspoon firmly packed brown sugar
- 1 tablespoon Irish whiskey
  Whipped cream, for garnish (optional)

1. In a 2-cup microwave-safe measure, microwave the water on high (100%) until boiling (2 to 2½ minutes).

2. To an Irish whiskey mug or coffee mug, add instant coffee and brown sugar. Pour boiling water into mug, stirring until instant coffee and brown sugar are dissolved.

3. Stir in whiskey. Top with dollop of whipped cream, if desired. Serve immediately.

Serves 1.

HOT SPICED CIDER

This delicious hot drink is best made with cider fresh from the cider mill. For extra zip, spike it with applejack, or let each guest add a shot of their favorite liquor.

- 8 whole cloves, stems attached
- 4 thin orange slices
- 4 cups apple cider
- 4 tablespoons firmly packed brown sugar
- 2 cinnamon sticks (3 in. each)

1. Insert 2 cloves into each orange slice. Set aside.

2. In a 2-quart microwave-safe measure, combine cider and brown sugar. Add cinnamon sticks. Float clove-studded orange slices on top. Cover and microwave on high (100%) 8 to 10 minutes, stirring once. Ladle into mugs and serve immediately.

Makes 4 cups, 4 servings.

SCOTCH CHOCOLATE

Butterscotch chips add a gourmet touch to hot chocolate.

- ¼ cup semisweet chocolate chips
- ¼ cup butterscotch chips
- 4 cups milk
- ¼ teaspoon ground cinnamon
- ½ teaspoon vanilla extract

1. In a 2-quart microwave-safe measure, combine chocolate and butterscotch chips. Microwave on high (100%) until chips are melted (1½ to 2 minutes), stirring twice. Do not overcook. Stir until smooth.

2. Add milk and cinnamon. Microwave on high until hot (4 to 6 minutes), stirring every minute. Do not boil. Stir in vanilla. Ladle into mugs and serve immediately.

Makes 4 cups, 4 servings.

BARTENDER'S SYRUP

The secret of professional bartenders is out! A simple syrup dissolves instantly, quickly sweetening mixed drinks and punches. This microwave version couldn't be easier.

- 2 cups sugar
- 1 cup water

1. In a 2-quart microwave-safe container, combine sugar and the water, stirring to mix. Microwave on high (100%) until mixture boils (4 to 6 minutes).

2. Cool and store covered in the refrigerator. Use in place of sugar in cold drinks.

Makes 1½ cups.

WASSAIL BOWL

Wassail comes from the Middle English words *waes haeil*, a friendly toast meaning "be thou well." This version is based on ale.

- 3 bottles (12 oz each) ale
- ½ cup firmly packed brown sugar
- 2 cinnamon sticks (3 in. each)
- 1 teaspoon whole cloves
- ½ teaspoon ground ginger
- 3 or 4 whole allspice
- 2 cups cream sherry

1. In a 4-quart microwave-safe container, combine 1 bottle of the ale, brown sugar, cinnamon sticks, cloves, ginger, and allspice. Microwave on high (100%) until mixture boils (2 to 3 minutes).

2. Add the remaining 2 bottles of ale and the sherry. Microwave on high until mixture boils again (2 to 3 minutes).

3. Reduce power to medium (50%) and microwave until hot (2 to 3 minutes). Serve in punch cups.

Makes 12 cups, 12 to 18 servings.

LEMON SYRUP

For a quick, refreshing glass of lemonade, many smart cooks prepare a concentrated syrup to store in the refrigerator. This easy microwave version generates no heat in the kitchen on a hot summer day. To make lemonade for 1, in a 12-ounce glass combine ½ cup syrup and ½ cup water. Fill glass with crushed ice and serve immediately.

> 1½ cups sugar
> 1½ cups water
> 1½ cups freshly squeezed lemon
>   juice (juice of 8 to 10 lemons)
>   Zest of 1 lemon, cut
>   into slivers

1. In a 3-quart microwave-safe dish, combine sugar and the water. Microwave on high (100%) until mixture boils and sugar dissolves (6 to 8 minutes), stirring every 2 minutes. Let cool completely.

2. Stir lemon juice and lemon zest into cooled syrup. Store covered in the refrigerator.

Makes 4 cups, 8 servings.

STRAWBERRY SHRUB

Early colonists used the plentiful wild berries they found to make drinks they called shrubs. Try using any berries in season for this refreshing drink. In the summer you might garnish the shrub with fresh mint leaves; in winter try adding rum. The quantity of liquid will vary depending upon the juiciness of the berries you select.

> 1 pint fresh strawberries or
>   1 package (10 oz) frozen
>   strawberries, defrosted
> ¼ cup sugar
> 3 tablespoons lemon juice
>   Cold water or club soda

1. Mash berries to a fine pulp. Let berries stand in their juice in refrigerator 4 to 6 hours or overnight.

2. Place mashed berries and juice in cheesecloth bag and let drain into a large microwave-safe bowl, pressing on bag to extract juice. Discard pulp.

3. Add sugar to berry juice; microwave on high (100%) until juice is hot and sugar is dissolved (2 to 3 minutes), stirring once. Stir in lemon juice.

4. Cover juice and place in refrigerator until chilled. For each serving measure ½ cup juice into a tall glass. Add ice and fill glass with cold water.

Makes about 2 cups, 4 servings.

This tempting Strawberry Shrub is a refreshing, old-fashioned iced drink for a hot summer day.

ORANGE-MINT ICED TEA

Make this refreshing treat when mint is plentiful in the herb garden. Try a delicious variation by substituting lemonade concentrate.

- 4   cups water
- 12   tea bags
- ¼   cup fresh mint leaves
- 1   can (6 oz) frozen orange juice concentrate
- 1   cup sugar

1. In a 4-quart microwave-safe container, combine the water, tea bags, and mint. Microwave on high (100%) until water boils (6 to 8 minutes). Let mixture stand 30 minutes. Strain.

2. Add orange juice concentrate and sugar. Stir.

3. Add enough tap water to make 8 cups liquid, then chill in refrigerator. Serve over ice.

Makes 8 cups, 8 servings.

HOT BUTTERED RUM

Rum lovers can enjoy this hot drink made with their favorite spirits.

- 6   cups water
- 3   tablespoons firmly packed brown sugar
- 3   tablespoons butter
- ½   teaspoon each *ground cinnamon, ground nutmeg, and ground cloves*
- 6   ounces rum
     Cinnamon sticks, for stirrers
- 4   lemon slices, for garnish

1. In a large microwave-safe glass measure, microwave the water on high (100%) until boiling (4 to 6 minutes).

2. In a small bowl cream brown sugar, butter, cinnamon, nutmeg, and cloves. Place 1 tablespoon of the mixture into each of 4 mugs.

3. Add 1½ ounces of the rum to each mug. Fill each mug with the hot water. Stir with cinnamon stick stirrer and float a lemon slice on top.

Serves 4.

HOT EGGNOG

This hot microwave eggnog is tasty sipped by a crackling fire.

- 4   cups milk
- 4   egg yolks
- ⅓   cup sugar
- ¼   teaspoon ground cinnamon, plus cinnamon for dusting
- ¼   teaspoon ground nutmeg
- ¼   teaspoon vanilla extract

1. In a 2-quart microwave-safe casserole, microwave milk on medium (50%) until hot but not boiling (4 to 6 minutes).

2. In a medium bowl beat egg yolks, sugar, cinnamon, nutmeg, and vanilla. Stir 1 cup of the hot milk into egg mixture. Gradually blend egg mixture into remaining milk.

3. Cover and microwave on medium until warm but not boiling (2 to 4 minutes), stirring once. Serve in mugs with dusting of cinnamon.

Makes 4 cups, 4 servings.

HOT CHOCOLATE

On frosty mornings delicious home-made chocolate mix encourages all family members to make their own microwave hot chocolate.

- 1   cup water
- 2   tablespoons Hot Chocolate Mix
     Marshmallow, for garnish (optional)

Hot Chocolate Mix

- 1   cup powdered nondairy creamer
- ¾   cup sugar
- ½   cup baking cocoa
- ¼   cup instant nonfat dry milk

In a coffee cup microwave the water on high (100%) until boiling (1½ to 2 minutes). Stir Hot Chocolate Mix into boiling water, mixing well. Top with marshmallow, if desired.

Serves 1.

Hot Chocolate Mix In a large bowl combine all ingredients, mixing thoroughly. Store in a tightly closed container.

Makes 2 cups mix, 32 servings.

HOT FUDGE FLOAT

Kids of all ages enjoy ice cream floats. The hot fudge makes this float a special microwave treat. Leftover hot fudge can be stored in a jar in the refrigerator for up to two weeks and used on ice cream (see page 97).

- ⅓   cup water
- 2   ounces unsweetened chocolate
- 1   tablespoon butter
- ¾   cup sugar
     Club soda
     Scoop ice cream

1. In a 2-cup microwave-safe glass measure, microwave the water, chocolate, and butter on high (100%) until chocolate and butter are melted (1½ to 2½ minutes), stirring once.

2. Stir in sugar and microwave on high 30 seconds. Stir and microwave on medium (50%) 30 seconds. Let stand 5 minutes.

3. To make float, place ice cubes in a 16-ounce glass and fill glass three quarters full with club soda. Float ice cream on soda and pour ¼ cup hot fudge over ice cream. Serve with a straw and long-handled spoon.

Serves 1.

MULLED WINE

This age-old treat is always good for sipping on a cold winter night.

- 1   bottle (1.5 liters) red table wine
- 3   cups apple juice
- 3   cinnamon sticks (3 in. each)
- 8   whole cloves
- 6   whole allspice

1. In a large microwave-safe container with a cover, combine wine and apple juice. Tie cinnamon sticks, cloves, and allspice in cheesecloth and place in wine. Cover and chill in refrigerator 2 to 4 hours.

2. Microwave container of wine on high (100%) until boiling (10 to 14 minutes). Let stand 10 minutes. Remove spice bag and ladle hot wine into mugs.

Makes 8 cups, 8 servings.

BREADS AND MUFFINS

Warm breads and muffins are a wonderful way to add a special accent to a meal. Coffee cakes and muffins made in the microwave are ready for breakfast or brunch in a minimum of time. Surprise your family with hot breads and muffins for lunch and dinner. They will appreciate the extra touch and you will appreciate the ease of microwave preparation.

APPLE MUFFINS

Muffins are a popular addition to any meal. Try these for a tasty breakfast treat, or serve them with a steaming mug of soup.

- ½ cup firmly packed brown sugar
- ⅓ cup vegetable oil
- 1 egg
- ½ cup milk
- 1 cup flour
- ½ teaspoon baking powder
- ½ teaspoon baking soda
- ¼ teaspoon salt
- 1 teaspoon ground cinnamon
- 1 cup chopped peeled apple

1. In a medium bowl combine brown sugar and oil. Beat in egg and milk. Add flour, baking powder, baking soda, salt, and cinnamon; stir until dry ingredients are just moistened. Gently fold in chopped apple.

2. Place paper liners in microwave-safe muffin dishes. Spoon batter into cups, filling half full.

3. Microwave 6 muffins at a time on high (100%) 2 to 4 minutes. Edges will be firm and centers slightly moist. Let stand 5 minutes. Repeat with remaining batter.

Makes 1 dozen muffins.

PEAR COFFEE CAKE

Reserving a portion of the dry ingredient mixture for the topping is an easy trick for quickly preparing streusel coffee cakes.

- 1 fresh pear, peeled, cored, and cut into ½-inch-thick slices (see Note)
- ½ cup butter or margarine
- 1 cup firmly packed brown sugar
- 1½ cups flour
- 1 cup milk
- 1 egg
- 1 teaspoon baking soda
- ¼ cup chopped walnuts
- ½ teaspoon ground nutmeg

1. Place pear slices on a microwave-safe plate. Cover and microwave on high (100%) until slices are easily pierced with a fork (1 to 2½ minutes). Set aside.

2. In a medium bowl cream butter and brown sugar. Add flour, mixing thoroughly. Reserve ¼ cup of the mixture for topping.

3. To remaining mixture add milk, egg, and baking soda; beat well. Stir in walnuts.

4. Lightly grease a 9-inch-diameter microwave-safe baking dish. Pour in batter. Place reserved pear slices decoratively on top of batter.

5. Add nutmeg to reserved topping and toss lightly. Sprinkle topping mixture over pear slices.

6. Microwave on medium-high (70%) until a toothpick inserted in center comes out clean (8 to 10 minutes), turning dish twice. Let stand directly on heatproof surface 10 minutes. Cut into wedges and serve warm.

Serves 6 to 8.

Note If fresh pears are not available, substitute 1 can (8 oz) sliced pears, drained, and eliminate step 1.

... ON REHEATING BAKED GOODS

Microwave ovens make quick work of warming baked goods, but the line between warm and hard or tough is very fine. Most beginning microwave cooks heat baked goods until they are steaming hot—only to discover that the baked goods are hard when ready to be served. For best results, baked goods should be heated only until they are slightly warm when touched. They will be hot and moist inside when served. Use the high (100%) power setting. The times given in the chart on page 33 are for reheating baked goods at room temperature.

☐ Loosely wrap rolls or bread in paper napkin or paper towel to absorb extra moisture during reheating. Moistureproof wrapping, such as waxed paper or plastic wrap, causes sogginess.

☐ Be careful with jelly-filled rolls or doughnuts. Filling will be hotter than baked goods.

☐ To warm a single frozen croissant, microwave on medium-low, or defrost setting (30%), 1 minute.

☐ For best reheating results with French or Italian bread, warm bread 6 slices at a time.

☐ Place custard cup of water in the microwave with stale bread or rolls. Steam will help to freshen them as they are reheated.

Whole Wheat Blueberry Muffins combine the nutrition of wheat and fruit for a delicious midmorning break with a piping-hot cup of tea.

WHOLE WHEAT BLUEBERRY MUFFINS

The addition of whole wheat flour adds nutritious fiber as well as the right touch of color to these blueberry muffins.

- ½ cup all-purpose flour
- ½ cup whole wheat flour
- 2 tablespoons sugar
- 2 teaspoons baking powder
- ½ teaspoon salt
- 1½ tablespoons butter
- 1½ tablespoons vegetable oil
- ½ cup milk
- 1 egg, slightly beaten
- ¾ cup fresh blueberries, rinsed and drained

1. In a medium bowl combine flours, sugar, baking powder, and salt. Make a well in the center.

2. In a 1-cup microwave-safe measure, microwave butter on high (100%) until melted (30 to 60 seconds). Add oil, milk, and egg; mix lightly and pour into well. Stir just enough to moisten dry ingredients. Gently fold in blueberries.

3. Place paper liners in microwave-safe muffin dishes. Spoon batter into cups, filling half full.

4. Microwave 6 muffins at a time on high 2 to 4 minutes. Edges will be firm and centers slightly moist. Let stand 5 minutes. Repeat with remaining batter.

Makes 1 dozen muffins.

BAKED GOODS REHEATING GUIDE

Reheating time is given in seconds and assumes the microwave is operating on high (100%) power.

Baked Goods	Amount	
	1 or 2	6
Rolls or muffins	10 to 15	30 to 40
Sweet rolls	10 to 15	30 to 40
Bagels	10 to 15	25 to 30
Bread slices	10 to 15	20 to 25
Doughnuts	10 to 15	20 to 25

SOUTH-OF-THE-BORDER CORN BREAD

Corn bread with the bite of jalapeño chiles is a perfect accompaniment for southwestern entrées. For a tasty snack any time of the day, slice left-over corn-bread squares crosswise, layer with cheese, and microwave on high (100%) 30 seconds or until the cheese is melted.

- 1 cup flour
- 1 cup cornmeal
- 1½ tablespoons baking powder
- ¼ cup sugar
- 1 cup milk
- 1 egg, slightly beaten
- 1 can (8 oz) corn, drained
- 3 or 4 jalapeño chiles, finely chopped

1. In a medium bowl combine flour, cornmeal, baking powder, and sugar. Stir in milk, egg, corn, and chiles until well mixed.

2. Pour batter into an 8-inch-diameter microwave-safe baking dish. Microwave on high (100%) until corn bread loosens from side of dish (7 to 9 minutes). Top may appear slightly moist in center. Let stand directly on heatproof surface 10 minutes, then cut into wedges and serve warm.

Serves 6.

CINNAMON CRUMB MUFFINS

These are a delicious treat piled in a basket on the brunch table.

- 1½ cups flour
- ½ cup sugar
- 2 teaspoons baking powder
- ½ teaspoon salt
- ¼ cup vegetable shortening
- ½ cup milk
- 1 egg, beaten

Crumb Topping

- ⅓ cup firmly packed brown sugar
- 2 tablespoons chopped walnuts
- 1 tablespoon flour
- 2 teaspoons ground cinnamon

1. In a large bowl combine flour, sugar, baking powder, and salt. Cut in shortening until mixture is crumbly. Make a well in the center.

2. In a small bowl combine milk and egg; pour into well. Stir just until dry ingredients are moistened.

3. Place paper liners in microwave-safe muffin dishes. Spoon batter into cups, filling half full. Sprinkle 1 heaping teaspoon Crumb Topping on each muffin. Microwave 6 muffins at a time on high (100%) until topping appears slightly moist (3 to 4 minutes).

Makes 1 dozen muffins.

Crumb Topping In a small bowl combine brown sugar, chopped walnuts, flour, and cinnamon; stir until well blended.

Makes about ⅓ cup.

QUICK BREAKFASTS

The morning rush hour may cause kitchen congestion. Teach family members to prepare their own breakfast choices in minutes with the microwave. If you prepare your favorite recipe for pancakes or waffles in advance, you can even enjoy them on a busy morning. Keep them in the freezer (stacked, separated by squares of waxed paper); reheat them on medium (50%) 1½ to 3½ minutes (for 1 or 2 pancakes or waffles) or 2½ to 5 minutes (for 3 or 4 pancakes or waffles).

FLUFFY SCRAMBLED EGG

Remember to slightly undercook an egg, since the heat in the egg continues to cook it as it is being served.

    1 egg
    1 tablespoon milk or water

In a small microwave-safe bowl, beat together egg and milk. Microwave on high (100%) 30 seconds. Stir and microwave again on high until egg is set (30 to 60 seconds).

Serves 1.

Egg to Go Follow the cooking instructions above, but use a 6- to 8-ounce insulating plastic cup as the cooking container and grab a plastic fork on the way out the door!

PERFECT POACHED EGG

For a perfect poached egg every time, remember the exact timing you find in step 2—when the yolk is slightly less cooked than the way you like it.

    ⅓ cup water
    1 egg

1. Place the water in a 1-cup microwave-safe casserole or custard cup. Cover and microwave on high (100%) until water begins to boil (1 to 2 minutes).

2. Break egg into boiling water. Cover and microwave on high until egg is set to your taste (30 to 60 seconds).

Serves 1.

CRISPY BACON

You do not have to use a browning tray to make crisp bacon. Just place the bacon on a paper towel (to absorb the excess grease) and microwave it until the bacon is cooked to your liking. Remember that bacon at room temperature cooks faster than bacon taken directly from the refrigerator.

    2 strips bacon

Place bacon strips side by side on a paper towel folded in half. Cover with a second paper towel. Microwave on high (100%) until bacon is as you like it: soft (1 to 2 minutes) or crisp (1½ to 3 minutes).

Serves 1.

OLD-FASHIONED OATMEAL

The microwave time is the same for quick-cooking and regular oatmeal, since both stand for 2 minutes after being cooked.

    ¼ cup quick-cooking or regular
      oatmeal
    ½ cup water

1. In a microwave-safe cereal bowl, combine oatmeal and the water. Microwave on high (100%) until mixture begins to boil (1 to 2 minutes).

2. Cover with saucer or waxed paper and let stand 2 minutes.

Serves 1.

CINNAMON-NUT COFFEE CAKE

Breakfast or brunch guests are delighted when greeted with warm pieces of coffee cake along with their morning coffee. If you make the coffee cake ahead, store it tightly wrapped. To reheat the whole coffee cake, cover it with a napkin or paper towel and microwave on high until it is just warm to the touch (1 to 1½ minutes).

    ¼ cup butter or margarine,
      softened (see page 87)
    1 cup sour cream
    1 egg, slightly beaten
    1½ cups flour
    ¾ cup sugar
    1 teaspoon baking powder
    ½ teaspoon baking soda
    1 teaspoon ground cinnamon

Cinnamon Streusel

    ¾ cup firmly packed brown
      sugar
    ½ cup chopped walnuts
    ½ teaspoon ground cinnamon

1. In medium mixer bowl combine butter and sour cream; beat until fluffy. Beat in egg.

2. Add flour, sugar, baking powder, baking soda, and cinnamon. Beat well. Spread batter in lightly greased 9-inch-diameter microwave-safe baking dish.

3. Sprinkle Cinnamon Streusel on top of batter. Microwave on medium-high (70%) 10 to 12 minutes. Let coffee cake stand directly on heatproof surface 15 minutes. Cut into wedges and serve warm.

Serves 6 to 8.

Cinnamon Streusel In a small bowl combine all ingredients. Stir until crumbly.

Makes about 1¼ cups.

GLAZED ORANGE MUFFINS

The glaze makes these nutritious breakfast muffins taste like sweet breakfast rolls.

- ¼ cup butter or margarine, softened
- ½ cup firmly packed brown sugar
- 1 egg, slightly beaten
- 1 tablespoon grated orange zest
- 1 cup flour
- 2 teaspoons baking powder
- ½ teaspoon salt
- ½ cup milk
- ½ teaspoon vanilla extract

Orange Glaze

- ½ cup sifted confectioners' sugar
- 2 tablespoons orange juice

1. In a large bowl cream butter and brown sugar until light and fluffy. Beat in egg and orange zest.

2. In a medium bowl sift together flour, baking powder, and salt. In a small bowl stir together milk and vanilla.

3. Alternately add flour mixture and milk mixture to butter mixture. Stir until dry ingredients are moistened.

4. Place paper baking liners in microwave-safe muffin dishes. Spoon batter into cups, filling halfway. Microwave 6 muffins at a time on high (100%) until tops appear dry (2½ to 3½ minutes). Repeat with remaining batter.

5. Remove muffins from dishes and set them on a waxed paper–covered cooling rack. Drizzle generously with Orange Glaze. Serve warm.

Makes 12 to 14 muffins.

Orange Glaze In a small bowl stir together confectioners' sugar and orange juice until mixture is smooth and well blended.

Makes about ¼ cup.

Special Feature

A NOT-SO-QUICK BREAKFAST

This omelet for one is simple to prepare when you want to treat yourself to a leisurely breakfast or brunch. Serve with orange juice, toast, and the morning paper.

SPANISH OMELET

- 2 teaspoons butter or margarine
- 2 tablespoons chopped green bell pepper
- 1 tablespoon chopped pimiento
- 1 tablespoon chopped onion
- 2 eggs
- 2 tablespoons milk
- ¼ teaspoon salt

1. In a 9-inch-diameter microwave-safe pie plate, combine 1 teaspoon of the butter, the pepper, pimiento, and onion. Microwave on high (100%) until vegetables are crisp-tender (2 to 3 minutes). Remove vegetables with a slotted spoon and set aside.

2. Add the remaining 1 teaspoon butter to pie plate. Microwave on high until butter is melted (30 to 60 seconds). In a small bowl combine eggs, milk, and salt; pour into pie plate. Microwave on high until edge of omelet begins to set (30 to 60 seconds). Stir, allowing liquid portion of omelet to run to outside of dish. Microwave on high until omelet is set (1½ to 2½ minutes).

3. Spoon reserved vegetables over half of omelet. Slide omelet onto a serving plate, folding omelet in half to cover vegetables. Serve hot.

Serves 1.

The light, creamy sauce clings delicately to the corkscrew pasta in Broccoli and Fusilli (see page 46), a colorful and appetizing vegetarian entrée.

Savory Side Dishes

I maginative side dishes are the
accessories that provide a menu
with color and variety of flavor.
Serve brilliant Southwestern Corn and Peppers
(see page 43) or colorful Wine-Braised Red
Cabbage (see page 46) to add visual interest to
a meal. Present a whole Curried Cauliflower
(see page 43) and earn rave reviews. The
colorful salads, tasty soups, and innovative
casseroles offered in this chapter enhance
any meal, yet are assertive enough
to stand alone.

VEGETABLES

Try one of these recipes when you need a side dish for a conventionally prepared meal as well as for a microwaved entrée. Most of the recipes can be prepared during the standing time of the microwaved entrée. In fact, the standing time for microwaved vegetables is usually never more than 5 minutes—the time it takes to serve them.

SPAGHETTI SQUASH WITH CHEESE SAUCE

Spaghetti-like strands inside this squash fascinate both children and adults. Select a firm squash with a hard rind and an unblemished surface. The squash keeps well for several weeks stored in a cool, dry place. For a different taste treat, follow the directions for cooking the squash through step 1 but serve the squash with spaghetti sauce or marinara sauce.

- 1 *medium spaghetti squash (about 3 lb)*
- 2 *tablespoons butter*
- 2 *tablespoons flour*
- ½ *teaspoon salt*
- 1 *cup milk*
- ¾ *cup grated Cheddar cheese*
- 1 *teaspoon Italian seasoning*
- ¼ *cup chopped parsley*
- 2 *tablespoons grated Parmesan cheese, for sprinkling*

1. Wash squash. With a sharp knife pierce skin in several places. Place on paper towel–covered microwave-safe plate. Microwave on high (100%) until squash yields to pressure when pressed with your fingertips (10 to 12 minutes). Set aside.

2. In a 2-cup microwave-safe measure, microwave butter on high until melted (1 to 1½ minutes). Add flour and salt, stirring to mix well. Pour

in milk and combine with flour mixture. Microwave on high 1 minute. Stir. Microwave again on high until sauce boils and thickens (1 to 2½ minutes), stirring twice. Add Cheddar cheese and microwave on high 1 minute. Stir until cheese is melted. Add Italian seasoning and parsley and stir to blend.

3. Cut baked squash in half crosswise. Scoop out and discard seeds. Scrape flesh with fork to separate into spaghetti-like strands. Place strands on serving platter, pour cheese sauce on top, and sprinkle with Parmesan. Serve immediately.

Serves 4.

ITALIAN STUFFED PEPPERS

Italian-style seasoning and summer vegetables are combined in this easy recipe. Serve as a side dish with grilled Italian sausage.

- 4 *medium green bell peppers*
- ¼ *cup water*
- 1 *tablespoon olive oil*
- 1 *tablespoon chopped fresh basil*
- 1 *clove garlic, minced*
- 1 *medium zucchini, peeled and shredded*
- 1½ *cups corn kernels*
- ½ *cup chopped pitted black olives*
- ½ *teaspoon salt*
- 2 *tablespoons grated Parmesan cheese, for sprinkling*

1. Wash peppers. Cut out tops and remove and discard seeds. Place in a 2-quart microwave-safe baking dish and add the water. Cover with waxed paper and microwave on high (100%) until crisp-tender (4 to 5 minutes), turning once. Drain in a colander and set aside.

2. In same casserole microwave oil on high until hot (1 to 2 minutes). Add basil and garlic. Microwave on high until garlic is soft (1 minute).

3. Add zucchini and corn. Cover and microwave on high until hot (4 to 5 minutes), stirring once. Stir in olives and salt.

4. Spoon vegetable mixture into cooked peppers. Place stuffed peppers in a circle in a 2-quart microwave-safe casserole. Sprinkle with cheese and microwave on high until heated (1 to 2 minutes). Let stand 5 minutes.

Serves 4.

BROCCOLI-STUFFED TOMATOES

Here is a fancy use for leftover rice that will impress your dinner guests. You might want to cook extra rice to have in the refrigerator just for making this dish.

- 4 *large ripe tomatoes*
  Salt and freshly ground pepper, for sprinkling
- 1½ *cups chopped fresh broccoli or 1 package (10 oz) frozen chopped broccoli*
- 1 *tablespoon water*
- 1 *cup cooked rice*
- 1 *cup shredded mozzarella cheese*
- 1 *teaspoon garlic salt*
- 2 *tablespoons minced onion*

1. Wash tomatoes, cut off tops, and scoop out pulp. Sprinkle cavity of each tomato with salt and pepper. Allow to drain upside down while preparing stuffing.

2. To a 2-quart microwave-safe casserole, add broccoli and the water. Cover and microwave on high (100%) until broccoli is hot (4 to 5 minutes), stirring once. Drain and return to casserole.

3. Add rice, cheese, garlic salt, and onion and mix well. Spoon broccoli mixture into tomato shells; place filled shells in a 9-inch-diameter microwave-safe baking dish.

4. Cover with waxed paper and microwave on high until tomatoes and stuffing are hot (4 to 6 minutes). Let stand, covered, 5 minutes.

Serves 4.

HOT SPINACH SALAD

The dressing of this salad was adapted from a German recipe for dressing used on tender spring dandelion greens. This microwave version is equally wonderful on fresh spinach.

- 10 ounces (about 4 cups) fresh spinach
- ½ teaspoon salt
- 1½ teaspoons sugar
- 2 or 3 green onions, thinly sliced
- 4 slices bacon
- 1 tablespoon flour
- ⅓ cup vinegar
- 2 hard-cooked eggs, peeled and sliced, for garnish

1. Thoroughly wash and dry spinach. Place in a salad bowl and sprinkle with salt, sugar, and green onion.

2. With kitchen shears cut bacon into 1-inch-long pieces; place in a 1-quart microwave-safe casserole. Microwave on high (100%) until bacon is crisp (2 to 3 minutes), stirring twice. Drain on paper towel, reserving 1 tablespoon of drippings in a small microwave-safe bowl.

3. Stir flour into reserved drippings until smooth. Microwave on high until bubbly (30 to 60 seconds). Stir in vinegar and microwave on high until boiling (1 to 2 minutes).

4. Pour vinegar mixture over spinach in salad bowl and toss to coat. Garnish with egg slices and reserved bacon pieces.

Serves 4.

Grill Italian sausage and your favorite polenta for the perfect accompaniment to these robust Italian Stuffed Peppers, filled with black olives, zucchini, and corn and seasoned with garlic and fresh basil.

MICROWAVE STIR-FRY

Stir-frying in a microwave is simple and fast and involves less stirring than cooking with a wok or skillet. Peanut oil is usually used for stir-frying, but you may substitute vegetable oil. For hints on using the microwave browning dish, see page 13.

BEEF WITH BROCCOLI

Stretch a half pound of beef round to serve four people a nutritious and filling Chinese meal. Freeze the meat for 30 minutes to make slicing easier. Complete the meal with a refreshing fruit sherbet of your choice and fortune cookies.

> ½ teaspoon sugar
> 2½ teaspoons cornstarch
> 1 tablespoon soy sauce
> ¼ teaspoon freshly ground pepper
> 1 tablespoon water
> ½ pound top round, cut into ¼-inch-thick slivers
> 3 tablespoons peanut oil
> 1 slice fresh ginger, peeled and minced
> 1 small onion, chopped
> 2 cloves garlic, minced
> 1½ cups broccoli florets
> 1 tablespoon oyster sauce
> 1 tablespoon dry sherry
> Hot cooked rice, for accompaniment

1. In a medium bowl combine sugar, 2 teaspoons of the cornstarch, the soy sauce, pepper, and the water. Add beef slivers and toss to coat. Let stand 15 minutes.

2. Preheat microwave browning dish on high (100%) 4 minutes. Swirl in 2 tablespoons of the peanut oil to coat surface of dish and microwave on high 1 minute. Add ginger, onion, and garlic. Microwave on high until onion mixture is slightly browned (30 to 45 seconds).

3. Stir in reserved beef mixture and microwave on high until beef is lightly browned (3 to 4 minutes), stirring twice. Remove beef and onion mixture to small dish and set aside.

4. Add remaining 1 tablespoon peanut oil to browning dish and swirl to coat. Microwave on high until hot (30 to 60 seconds). Add broccoli and microwave on high until broccoli just begins to brown (1 to 2 minutes). Stir in oyster sauce, sherry, and remaining ½ teaspoon cornstarch. Cover with lid and microwave on high until broccoli is crisp-tender (3 to 5 minutes), stirring every minute.

5. Add reserved beef and onion mixture, stirring to combine. Microwave on high until mixture is hot (1 to 2 minutes). Serve immediately with hot cooked rice.

Serves 3 to 4.

STIR-FRIED SNOW PEAS AND MUSHROOMS

Look for *shiitake* mushrooms in an Asian grocery or the Asian food section of your supermarket. Their dark hue provides a striking color contrast to the snow peas, as shown in the photograph on page 41.

> 5 to 7 shiitake mushrooms
> 1 tablespoon peanut oil
> ½ pound fresh snow peas or 1 package (8 oz) frozen snow peas
> 2 green onions, sliced
> 1 slice fresh ginger, peeled and minced
> ½ cup chicken stock
> 1½ teaspoons cornstarch
> 1 teaspoon sugar
> 1 teaspoon soy sauce

1. Place mushrooms in a small bowl and add enough water to cover. Let stand until mushrooms are softened (about 10 minutes).

2. In a 2-quart microwave-safe dish, microwave peanut oil on high

(100%) until hot (1 to 1½ minutes). Add snow peas, green onion, and ginger. Cover and microwave on high until peas are crisp-tender (3 to 5 minutes), stirring twice.

3. Drain softened mushrooms (reserving liquid for another use); cut mushrooms into ¼-inch-thick slivers and stir into snow pea mixture.

4. In a small bowl combine stock, cornstarch, sugar, and soy sauce. Stir into snow pea and mushroom mixture. Microwave on high until mixture is hot and liquid is slightly thickened (2 to 3 minutes). Serve immediately.

Serves 4 to 5.

STIR-FRIED SESAME BEANS

Try the stir-fry method with these green beans for a super side dish served with either a Western- or Asian-style dinner.

> 3 teaspoons peanut oil
> 1 tablespoon sesame seed
> 1 pound fresh green beans, washed and trimmed
> 1 small onion, finely chopped
> 1 tablespoon water
> ¼ teaspoon sesame oil
> 1 teaspoon soy sauce

1. In a 1½-quart microwave-safe casserole, microwave 1 teaspoon of the peanut oil on high (100%) until hot (30 to 60 seconds). Add sesame seed, stirring to coat with oil. Microwave on high until seed is toasted (2 to 3 minutes). Remove seed and set aside.

2. Add the remaining 2 teaspoons peanut oil to casserole. Microwave on high until hot (30 to 60 seconds). Stir in green beans and onion. Microwave on high 1 to 2 minutes. Stir. Add the water, cover, and microwave on high until beans are crisp-tender (5 to 6 minutes).

3. Add sesame oil, soy sauce, and reserved sesame seed. Toss to mix. Serve immediately.

Serves 4 or 5.

KUNG PAO CHICKEN

This popular Chinese dish (at left in the photograph above) can be even hotter if you increase the amount of dried chiles. Because the oil in the chiles may cause a burning sensation on your skin, wash your hands after handling them.

1 chicken breast (about ¾ lb), skin removed, cut into ½-inch cubes
2 teaspoons cornstarch
½ cup plus 1 tablespoon water
½ teaspoon sugar
2 tablespoons peanut oil
1 slice fresh ginger, peeled and minced
1 green onion, sliced
2 cloves garlic, minced
3 dried red chiles, broken into small pieces
½ cup sliced carrots
½ cup cauliflower florets
½ cup unsalted dry-roasted peanuts
Hot cooked rice, for accompaniment

Flavoring Sauce

¼ teaspoon sugar
½ teaspoon cornstarch
2 teaspoons dry sherry
1 teaspoon sesame oil
1 tablespoon soy sauce
1 tablespoon water

1. In a medium bowl combine chicken, cornstarch, 1 tablespoon of the water, and sugar, tossing to coat. Let stand 15 minutes.

2. Preheat microwave browning dish on high (100%) 4 minutes. Swirl in 1 tablespoon of the peanut oil to coat surface of dish and microwave on high 1 minute. Add ginger, green onion, garlic, and chiles. Microwave on high until onion is soft (30 to 45 seconds).

3. Add chicken mixture and stir to coat with oil mixture. Microwave on high until chicken is no longer pink (3 to 5 minutes), stirring every minute. Remove chicken to a small bowl and reserve.

4. Add remaining 1 tablespoon peanut oil to browning dish and swirl to coat. Microwave on high until hot (30 to 60 seconds). Add carrots, cauliflower, and ½ cup of the water. Cover with lid and microwave on high until vegetables are crisp-tender (3 to 4 minutes), stirring twice. Stir in Flavoring Sauce and microwave until sauce is slightly thickened (1 to 2 minutes).

5. Stir in peanuts and reserved chicken; microwave on high until chicken is hot (1 to 2 minutes). Serve immediately with hot cooked rice.

Serves 3 to 4.

Flavoring Sauce In a small bowl combine all ingredients.

Makes about 3 tablespoons.

Cumin adds a distinctive southwestern flavor to this zesty, colorful combination of corn, onion, and red and green bell pepper.

APPLESAUCE AND SQUASH

Fall produces an abundance of apples and squash. Their flavors complement each other in this delicious cool-weather dish.

    2   small acorn squash
    1   cup applesauce
    4   teaspoons butter or margarine
        Freshly ground nutmeg, for
        sprinkling

1. Wash squash and pierce skin. Place on a microwave-safe plate and microwave on high (100%) until squash feels tender when pressure is applied with your fingertip (12 to 14 minutes), turning squash over halfway through cooking time.

2. Cut each squash in half lengthwise; scoop out and discard seeds. Return squash halves to plate. In the cavity of each, place ¼ cup of the applesauce and 1 teaspoon of the butter. Sprinkle with nutmeg.

3. Microwave on high until applesauce is hot (2 to 3 minutes). Serve immediately.

Serves 4.

SOUTHWESTERN CORN AND PEPPERS

Corn, red and green bell peppers, and cumin are all popular ingredients in southwestern cooking. Combining these ingredients produces a tasty side dish with a Mexican flavor that adds zest to any meal.

> 3 cups corn kernels
> 1 small green bell pepper, chopped
> 1 small red bell pepper, chopped
> ½ cup chopped onion
> 1 tablespoon butter or margarine
> ½ teaspoon ground cumin
> ½ teaspoon salt
> ¼ teaspoon freshly ground pepper

1. In a 2-quart microwave-safe casserole, combine corn, bell pepper, onion, and butter. Cover and microwave on high (100%) until bell pepper is crisp-tender (5 to 7 minutes), stirring once.

2. Stir in cumin, salt, and ground pepper. Cover and let stand 5 minutes before serving.

Serves 4.

LEMON-BUTTERED GREEN BEANS

Lemon adds zing to green beans, making them a delicious addition to any meal. Lemon butter is especially tasty with fresh beans in season, but you can also use this flavor trick with frozen beans.

> 1 pound fresh green beans, trimmed and washed or 1 package (9 oz) frozen cut green beans
> 2 tablespoons water
> 1 tablespoon butter
> 1 tablespoon lemon juice
> ¼ teaspoon freshly ground pepper

1. In a 1½-quart microwave-safe casserole, combine green beans and the water. Cover and microwave on high (100%) until beans are crisp-tender (5 to 6 minutes).

2. Add butter, lemon juice, and pepper. Cover and microwave on high until butter is melted (1 to 2 minutes). Toss to mix and serve immediately.

Serves 4 or 5.

CURRIED CAULIFLOWER

Guests are eager to try food that looks appetizing. A whole cauliflower is a superb meal presentation made easy in your microwave oven.

> 1 medium head cauliflower, washed and trimmed

Curry Sauce

> ½ cup yogurt or sour cream
> 1 tablespoon mayonnaise
> 1½ teaspoons curry powder
> ½ teaspoon salt
> ¼ teaspoon freshly ground pepper

1. Remove core from cauliflower, leaving head whole. Place in a microwave-safe casserole or dish and cover with waxed paper. Microwave on high (100%) until florets are crisp-tender when pierced with a fork

(11 to 13 minutes). Let stand, covered, 5 minutes.

2. Place cooked cauliflower head on a serving plate and pour Curry Sauce on top. Serve immediately.

Serves 4.

Curry Sauce In a 1-cup microwave-safe measure, combine yogurt, mayonnaise, curry, salt, and pepper. Microwave on medium (50%) until sauce is warm but not bubbling (1½ to 2½ minutes), stirring once.

Makes about ½ cup.

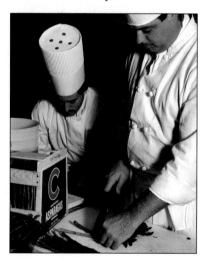

BLANCHING VEGETABLES FOR FREEZING

When your garden is producing armloads of fresh produce, you will appreciate your microwave oven. To carry you through the less prolific months, pick vegetables as they ripen and blanch them in small batches for freezing without heating up your kitchen on a hot summer day.

1. Prepare vegetables as you would for conventional blanching.

2. Place 1 pound of vegetables in a 2-quart microwave-safe casserole.

3. Add ⅓ cup water. Do not add salt.

4. Cover and microwave on high (100%) according to time given in the chart on page 43. Stir vegetables halfway through cooking time.

5. Drain vegetables in colander and plunge into ice water. Stir to cool and to stop cooking.

6. Package vegetables immediately, label, and place in freezer.

FRENCH STEAMED PEAS

The French treat fresh peas with a minimum of fuss, preferring to keep them simple. The shredded lettuce, which provides just the right amount of moisture for perfect steaming, is a tasty accompaniment to the sweet peas.

    1 tablespoon butter or
      margarine
    ¾ cup shredded washed lettuce
      leaves
    3 cups shelled fresh peas
    1 tablespoon water
    1 teaspoon sugar
    ¼ teaspoon freshly ground
      pepper

1. In a 1½-quart microwave-safe casserole, microwave butter on high (100%) until it is melted (30 to 60 seconds).

2. Add lettuce, peas, the water, and sugar. Cover and microwave on high until peas are tender (5 to 7 minutes). Let stand, covered, 5 minutes. Sprinkle with pepper and serve.

Serves 4.

CARROT-ZUCCHINI MEDLEY

The julienne cut of the carrots and zucchini allows the vegetables to cook quickly and evenly. Use the zucchini unpeeled to add an extra touch of color to this popular, eye-pleasing dish.

    3 tablespoons butter or
      margarine
    3 cups julienned zucchini
      (about 3 medium)
    3 cups julienned carrots
      (about 3 medium)
    ½ teaspoon salt
    ¼ teaspoon freshly ground
      pepper
    ¼ teaspoon dried oregano

1. In a 3-quart microwave-safe casserole, combine butter, zucchini, and carrots. Cover and microwave on high (100%) until vegetables are crisp-tender (5 to 7 minutes), stirring twice.

2. Add salt, pepper, and oregano. Toss to coat zucchini mixture with seasonings, then cover and let stand 5 minutes before serving.

Serves 4.

BROCCOLI-CAULIFLOWER TOSS

Broccoli and cauliflower make an attractive color combination when served together in this nutritious dish. Cut these two vegetables into florets of similar size for even cooking.

    2 tablespoons butter or
      margarine
    ¼ teaspoon garlic salt
    ⅛ teaspoon freshly ground
      pepper
    1 medium head broccoli, cut
      into florets
    1 small head cauliflower, cut
      into florets

1. In a 1-cup microwave-safe measure, combine butter, garlic salt, and pepper. Microwave on high (100%) until butter is melted (15 to 30 seconds), then stir to thoroughly combine.

2. Place broccoli and cauliflower florets in a 2-quart microwave-safe casserole. Pour melted butter mixture over vegetables and toss to coat. Cover and microwave on high until vegetables are crisp-tender (6 to 8 minutes). Let stand, covered, 5 minutes before serving.

Serves 6.

MICROWAVING FRESH VEGETABLES

Cooking time is given in minutes and assumes the vegetable is covered and the microwave is operating on high (100%) power. Standing time is minimum and is given in minutes.

Vegetable	Amount	Approximate Cooking Time	Standing Time
Artichokes	1 (6 to 8 oz)	5 to 8	5
	2	8 to 10	5
	4	12 to 14	5
Asparagus (Pare stalks except on very thin spears)	1 lb; 2 tbsp water	4 to 7	1
Beans, green or wax Cut into 1½-in. pieces	1 lb; 2 tbsp water	5 to 7	2
Beets, whole	1½ lb; 2 cups water	14 to 16	2
Broccoli Cut into spears (pare stalks)	1 lb; 2 tbsp water	5 to 7	2
Brussels sprouts	1 tub (10 oz); 1 tbsp water	5 to 7	2
	1 lb; 2 tbsp water	8 to 10	3
Cabbage Chopped or shredded	4 cups (about 1 lb); 2 tbsp water	6 to 8	0
Wedges	4 (about 1 lb); 2 tbsp water	5 to 7	2
Carrots, sliced into rounds	1 lb; 2 tbsp water	6 to 8	1
Cauliflower Cut into florets	1 lb; 2 tbsp water	6 to 8	2
Whole	1 to 1½ lb; 2 tbsp water	11 to 13	3
Corn on the cob	1 ear	3 to 4	3
	2 ears	4 to 5	3
	4 ears	8½ to 10	3
Eggplant Cubed	1 lb; 2 tbsp water	6 to 8	1
Whole (pierce skin)	1 to 1¼ lb	4 to 7	3
Onions Small, whole	1 lb; 2 tbsp water	4 to 8	2
Okra	1 lb; ⅓ cup water	7 to 9	2
Parsnips, sliced	1 lb; 2 tbsp water	6 to 8	2
Peas, green	1½ lb; 3 tbsp water	5 to 7	1
Peas, snow (pea pods)	1 lb; 2 tbsp water	4 to 6	1
Potatoes, new Small, whole (pierce skin)	1 lb (6 to 8); 3 tbsp water	8 to 12	3
Potatoes, white or sweet Whole for baking (pierce skin)	1 (6 to 8 oz)	4 to 6	5
	2	6 to 9	5
	4	12 to 14	5
Spinach Washed, whole leaves	1 lb (water that clings to leaves is enough moisture)	4 to 6	0
Squash, spaghetti Whole (pierce skin)	1 (3 to 5 lb)	10 to 14	5
Squash, summer	1 lb; 2 tbsp water	4 to 6	0
Squash, winter Whole (pierce skin)	1 (1 lb)	6 to 8	5
	2 (¾ lb each)	7 to 9	5
Turnips	1 lb; ¼ cup water	7 to 9	5
Zucchini, sliced ½ in. thick	1 lb; 2 tbsp water	4 to 6	0

MICROWAVING POTATOES AND PASTA

Cooking potatoes and pasta in the microwave is sometimes confusing. Just remember that when boiling these foods, they often require cooking times similar to those needed in conventional cooking to heat the water, and if you increase the amount of food, you also need to increase the cooking time. These suggestions should help you make the necessary adjustments.

BAKED POTATOES

Potatoes baked in the microwave can be a real time and energy saver. Select white or sweet potatoes of uniform medium size so all will cook evenly in the same amount of time. Scrub potatoes and prick skin with a fork. Cover a microwave-safe plate with a layer of paper toweling. Arrange potatoes in a spoke design, with the smaller ends toward the center. Microwave on high (100%) according to the chart on page 47. Wrap potatoes and allow them to stand 5 minutes before serving: Wrapping them in aluminum foil during standing produces soft skins; for drier skins wrap them in a paper or cloth towel. Placing the potatoes in a conventional or toaster oven for a few minutes crisps the skins.

BOILED POTATOES

Peel potatoes. Leave small potatoes whole and cut medium or large potatoes into quarters; pieces should be of uniform size for even cooking. Place in a microwave-safe casserole with ½ cup water and ½ teaspoon salt, if desired. Cover and microwave on high (100%) according to the chart on page 47. More than 4 potatoes may be cooked in the microwave by boiling longer, but the cooking time may be similar to that of conventional cooking.

PASTA

The cooking times are similar for microwave and conventional methods of cooking pasta, but many cooks prefer the perfect al dente texture and easy cleanup that the microwave offers. If that sounds appealing, here are some guidelines.

PERFECT PASTA

Select the cooking container according to the pasta shape. Long, thin pastas—such as spaghetti, lasagne, or fettuccine—cook perfectly in an 8- by 12- by 2-inch dish. Smaller pasta shapes—such as bowties, shells, elbows, corkscrews, or ziti—microwave best in a deep 3- or 4-quart casserole. To reheat pasta, see Note.

4 to 6 cups hot water
1 tablespoon vegetable oil
¼ teaspoon salt
8 ounces pasta

In a microwave-safe casserole best suited to the shape of the pasta you are cooking, combine the water, oil, and salt. Cover and microwave on high (100%) until water boils (8 to 10 minutes). Add pasta. Cover and microwave on high until pasta is tender (6 to 10 minutes). Let stand, covered, 2 to 3 minutes. Drain, rinse, and serve immediately.

Note To reheat pasta in the microwave, add 1 teaspoon water per cup of cooked pasta. Cover and microwave on medium-high (70%) until pasta is steaming (1 to 2 minutes per cup), stirring once. Let stand, covered, 2 minutes before serving.

WINE-BRAISED RED CABBAGE

This popular German dish is especially good in cool weather when served with roast pork or beef.

1 small head red cabbage (about 2 lb), cored and shredded
1 green apple, peeled, cored, and chopped
1 small onion, thinly sliced
½ cup dry red wine
2 tablespoons firmly packed brown sugar
½ teaspoon salt
¼ teaspoon freshly ground pepper

1. In a 3-quart microwave-safe casserole, combine cabbage, apple, onion, wine, and brown sugar. Cover and microwave on high (100%) until cabbage is crisp-tender (8 to 10 minutes).

2. Stir in salt and pepper. Cover and let stand 5 minutes before serving.

Serves 6.

BROCCOLI AND FUSILLI

The curly twists of *fusilli* cling well to the chopped vegetables in this pasta and vegetable dish, which can be served as a vegetarian entrée.

1 box (16 oz) fusilli
2 tablespoons butter or margarine
1 pound fresh mushrooms, cleaned and sliced
1½ cups chopped fresh broccoli or 1 package (10 oz) frozen chopped broccoli
1 cup seeded and chopped fresh tomatoes
¾ cup half-and-half
2 teaspoons chopped fresh basil
½ teaspoon dried oregano
¼ cup grated Parmesan cheese
½ teaspoon salt
Freshly ground pepper, to taste

1. Cook fusilli conventionally, according to package directions. Drain.

2. Meanwhile, in a 3-quart microwave-safe casserole, microwave butter on high (100%) until melted (30 to 60 seconds). Add mushrooms and microwave on high 1 minute. Stir. Add broccoli, tomatoes, half-and-half, basil, and oregano. Microwave on high 2 minutes. Stir and microwave on medium (50%) until broccoli is crisp-tender (3 to 4 minutes).

3. Place cooked fusilli in a serving bowl. Add vegetable sauce, cheese, salt, and pepper. Mix well and serve immediately.

Serves 4.

CREAMED ONIONS AND PEAS

Spring brings visions of fresh new peas and little pearl onions. Cook them quickly in the microwave and serve them in this easy lump-free cream sauce.

- *½ pound small pearl onions, peeled*
- *¼ cup water*
- *2 tablespoons butter or margarine*
- *2 tablespoons flour*
- *½ teaspoon salt*
- *1 cup evaporated milk*
- *1 cup shelled green peas*

1. To a 2-quart microwave-safe casserole, add onions and the water. Cover and microwave on high (100%) until onions are tender (5 to 7 minutes). Drain in colander and set aside.

2. Add butter to same casserole and microwave on high until butter melts (1 to 1½ minutes). Add flour and salt, stirring until smooth. Add milk

and stir to combine with flour mixture. Microwave on high 1 minute. Stir, then microwave again on high until sauce boils and thickens (1 to 2½ minutes), stirring twice.

3. Add peas and cooked onions. Cover and microwave on high until vegetables are hot (1 to 2 minutes). Serve immediately.

Serves 4.

EASY POTATOES AU GRATIN

Cheddar cheese soup gives these potatoes their cheesy taste. Serve with meat loaf and a salad for a real grass-roots American-style meal.

- *4 medium potatoes, scrubbed*
- *½ cup diced celery*
- *1 small onion, chopped*
- *1 can (10½ oz) condensed Cheddar cheese soup*
- *1 tablespoon prepared mustard Paprika, for sprinkling*

1. Place potatoes in a circle on a paper towel–covered microwave-safe plate, with small ends toward the center of plate. Pierce potatoes with a fork. Microwave on high (100%) until potatoes are still slightly firm (6 to 10 minutes). Cool 10 minutes, then cut each potato into ¼-inch-thick slices.

2. In a 2-quart microwave-safe casserole, combine potato slices, celery, onion, soup, and mustard. Cover and microwave on high until potatoes are hot and celery is crisp-tender (3 to 5 minutes), stirring once.

3. Let stand, covered, 5 minutes. Sprinkle with paprika and serve.

Serves 4 or 5.

BAKED POTATO GUIDE	
Number of Potatoes	**Time**
1	4 to 6 minutes
2	6 to 9 minutes
3	9 to 12 minutes
4	12 to 14 minutes
5	13 to 16 minutes
6	14 to 18 minutes

BOILED POTATO GUIDE	
Number of Potatoes	**Time**
1	6 to 7½ minutes
2	7 to 8½ minutes
3	8 to 9½ minutes
4	9 to 10½ minutes

CELERY PARMESAN

Celery is often forgotten as a vegetable to be served on its own. Frequently used in other dishes, it's delicious when prepared simply and served alone. Look for bunches of celery with fresh leaves and firm, crisp stalks that snap easily.

- *4 or 5 tender inner stalks celery, leaves removed*
- *2 tablespoons water*
- *½ teaspoon salt*
- *½ cup grated Parmesan cheese, for sprinkling*

1. Trim celery and cut into 1½-inch-long pieces.

2. Place celery pieces in a 1½-quart microwave-safe casserole. Add the water and salt. Cover and microwave on high (100%) until celery is crisp-tender (4 to 5 minutes), stirring once. Drain celery.

3. Sprinkle celery with cheese and toss to coat. Let stand, covered, 5 minutes before serving.

Serves 4.

SOUPS

Soup can be an elegant first course, a hearty or light lunch or dinner, and a surprising dessert. These recipes demonstrate the versatility of soup and allow you to experiment with many presentations.

FAST FRENCH ONION SOUP

French onion soup usually requires long, slow cooking to develop flavor. This microwave version can be prepared on short notice. Use a rich beef stock to enhance the flavor.

1½ cups thinly sliced sweet onions
    or yellow onions (about
    2 large)
  3 tablespoons butter
  6 cups beef stock
  ¼ teaspoon ground pepper
1½ tablespoons dry sherry
  4 slices French bread, toasted
  4 slices Swiss cheese

1. In a 3-quart microwave-safe dish, combine onions and butter. Microwave on high (100%) until onions are very soft and limp (5 to 7 minutes), stirring twice.

2. Add stock and pepper. Microwave on high until boiling (6 to 10 minutes). Stir in sherry.

3. Ladle soup into 4 microwave-safe soup crocks. Top each crock with a slice of toast and cheese. Microwave 4 crocks on high until cheese is melted (1 to 2 minutes). Serve hot.

Makes 4 to 5 cups, 4 servings.

CHEESY CORN CHOWDER

Thick hot chowders are welcome when cool breezes blow. Serve this one with a tossed salad and crisp bread sticks for an easy lunch or a light supper.

  2 tablespoons butter or
    margarine
  1 small onion, chopped
  2 tablespoons flour
  3 cups milk
  3 cups corn kernels
1½ cups shredded Cheddar cheese
1½ teaspoons salt
  ¼ teaspoon ground pepper

1. In a 4-quart microwave-safe casserole, combine butter and onion. Cover and microwave on high (100%) until onion is soft (1½ to 2 minutes). Sprinkle with flour, stirring to combine.

2. Stir in 1 cup of the milk. Cover and microwave on high until mixture is thickened (2 to 3 minutes), stirring every minute.

3. Add the remaining 2 cups milk, corn, cheese, salt, and pepper. Cover and microwave on medium (50%) until chowder is hot but not boiling (2 to 3 minutes). Ladle into bowls and serve immediately.

Makes 4 to 5 cups, 4 servings.

CURRIED ZUCCHINI SOUP

This lovely green soup looks tempting in the summer served cold in a clear iced soup bowl and garnished with a floating nasturtium. Served hot (see Note), it is also a hearty winter soup, so make extra when zucchini is plentiful and store the soup in the freezer.

2 pounds zucchini
1 cup chicken stock
2 tablespoons butter or
  margarine
¼ teaspoon salt
1 teaspoon curry powder
1 cup half-and-half

1. Wash zucchini and cut into very thin slices. In a 2-quart microwave-safe casserole, combine zucchini slices, stock, and butter. Cover and microwave on high (100%) until zucchini is very soft (7 to 10 minutes), stirring twice.

2. Place cooked zucchini in the work bowl of a food processor. Add salt, curry, and half-and-half. Process until mixture is puréed (30 to 45 seconds). Chill at least 3 hours before serving.

Makes 4 cups, 4 servings.

Note To serve hot, return puréed mixture to microwave casserole. Microwave on medium (50%) until soup is hot but not boiling (3 to 5 minutes). Serve immediately.

APPLE GINGER SOUP

This delicious apple soup is versatile enough to be served as a first course or as dessert.

4 medium tart apples, peeled,
  cored, and chopped, plus
  1 apple, unpeeled and
  chopped, for garnish
4 cups chicken stock
2 slices fresh ginger, chopped
  Salt, to taste

1. In a 3-quart microwave-safe casserole, combine chopped peeled apples, stock, and ginger. Cover and microwave on high (100%) until soup is boiling and apples are very soft (10 to 12 minutes).

2. Process soup in the work bowl of a food processor or blender until apples are puréed. Return soup to microwave casserole.

3. Taste soup, season with salt, and microwave on high until soup is hot (2 to 3 minutes). Ladle into soup bowls and garnish with unpeeled chopped apple.

Makes 4 cups, 4 servings.

VEGETABLE BARLEY SOUP

Here is a hearty, stick-to-the-ribs soup that is a favorite with children.

1 cup water
½ cup barley
2 carrots, scraped and diced
2 tablespoons butter
1 stalk celery, washed and diced
1 large onion, chopped
2 cloves garlic, minced
4 cups rich chicken stock
1 teaspoon dried oregano
  Salt and pepper, to taste

1. In a 2-cup microwave-safe measure, microwave the water on high (100%) until boiling (2 to 3 minutes). Stir in barley. Microwave on high 2 to 3 minutes. Cover and let stand 10 minutes.

2. To a 3-quart microwave-safe casserole, add carrots. Cover and microwave on high 2 minutes. Add butter, celery, onion, and garlic. Cover and microwave on high until vegetables are soft (3 to 5 minutes).

3. Add cooked barley, stock, and oregano. Cover and microwave on high until boiling (5 to 7 minutes). Season with salt and pepper. Let stand, covered, 10 minutes.

Makes 4 to 5 cups, 4 or 5 servings.

FRESH TOMATO BISQUE

Make this soup when vegetable markets are piled high with flavorful, ripe red tomatoes.

    2 *pounds ripe tomatoes*
    4 *cups chicken stock*
    2 *tablespoons butter*
    1 *small onion, chopped*
    2 *tablespoons flour*
   ½ *teaspoon dried thyme*
    1 *bay leaf*
      Sugar, to taste
      Salt and freshly ground pepper, to taste
      Sprigs fresh thyme, for garnish (optional)

1. Wash and quarter tomatoes. In a 4-quart microwave-safe casserole, combine tomatoes and stock. Cover and microwave on high (100%) until tomatoes are soft (10 to 14 minutes), stirring twice. (Time depends on ripeness of tomatoes.) Crush and strain cooked tomatoes through food mill or sieve; reserve tomato stock.

2. In same casserole combine butter and onion. Microwave on high until onion is soft (2 to 3 minutes). Stir in flour and microwave on high 1 minute. Add 1 cup of the reserved tomato stock and microwave until mixture is slightly thickened (1 to 2 minutes), stirring once. Add remaining reserved tomato stock, thyme, and bay leaf. Season with sugar, salt, and pepper.

3. Cover and microwave on high until hot (3 to 5 minutes). Ladle soup into bowls, garnish with sprigs of fresh thyme (if desired), and serve immediately.

Makes 4 to 5 cups, 4 or 5 servings.

A perfect nasturtium blossom is the colorful garnish for this bowl of exotic Curried Zucchini Soup. Depending on the weather, this flavorful soup can be served hot or chilled.

... FOR SOUPS AND VEGETABLES

Here are some helpful suggestions you can use to make soup and vegetable preparation a snap in the microwave oven.

☐ A 4-cup microwave-safe measuring cup is an ideal container for heating soups.

☐ Heat single servings of soup right in the bowl for easy cleanup. Microwave a cup of water to make instant soups.

☐ Heat milk- or cream-based soups on medium (50%) to prevent boiling over.

☐ When combining vegetable medleys, check the chart about microwaving fresh vegetables (see page 45) and choose ingredients with similar cooking times.

☐ Cut vegetables into similar-sized pieces for even cooking.

☐ Vegetables cooked in their skins, such as potatoes and squash, should be pierced with a fork before cooking and do not need to be covered during cooking. Cook all other vegetables covered to retain moisture and steam for quick, even cooking.

☐ Cook vegetables on high (100%).

☐ Stir vegetables once during microwaving to distribute heat for even cooking.

☐ Add salt to vegetables after cooking is completed. Add all other seasonings before cooking.

AVGOLEMONO

The tart lemon flavor of this Greek soup sharpens the taste buds for the dishes that follow.

> 3 cups chicken stock
> 1 cup cooked rice
> 2 tablespoons butter
> 3 egg yolks
> 3 tablespoons lemon juice
> Chopped parsley, for garnish

1. In a 3-quart microwave-safe casserole, combine 2 cups of the chicken stock, rice, and butter. Cover and microwave on high (100%) until stock is hot (6 to 8 minutes).

2. In a 2-cup microwave-safe measure, microwave the remaining 1 cup stock on high until boiling (2 to 3 minutes). In a small bowl beat egg yolks until light and fluffy. Gradually beat in lemon juice and the 1 cup hot stock.

3. Gently stir egg yolk mixture into cooked rice. Cover soup and let stand 5 minutes. Ladle into bowls and garnish with parsley.

Makes 4 cups, 4 servings.

VICHYSSOISE

Vichyssoise is traditionally served very cold in a chilled cup set in a bed of crushed ice.

> 4 medium potatoes, peeled and cut into ½-inch chunks
> 3 medium leeks, white part only, cut into ½-inch chunks
> 1 medium onion, chopped
> 3 tablespoons butter
> 3 cups rich chicken stock
> 1 cup milk
> 1 cup whipping cream
> ½ teaspoon salt
> ¼ teaspoon ground pepper
> Crushed ice, for serving soup
> Chopped chives, for garnish

1. In a 4-quart microwave-safe casserole, combine potatoes, leeks, onion, butter, and ½ cup of the stock. Microwave on high (100%) 5 minutes, stirring once. Add the remaining 2½ cups stock. Cover and microwave on high until potatoes and leeks are soft (12 to 14 minutes).

2. Force mixture through a food mill or process in the work bowl of a food processor, retaining coarse texture (5 to 10 seconds). Return to microwave casserole.

3. Add milk, cream, salt, and pepper. Cover soup and chill in the refrigerator. Serve in bowls set in crushed ice and garnished with chopped chives.

Makes 4 to 5 cups, 4 servings.

HOT AND SOUR SOUP

This favorite Chinese soup is a delicious beginning for a Chinese meal.

> 4 dried whole shiitake mushrooms
> 1 cup boiling water
> 3 cups chicken stock
> 1 tablespoon soy sauce
> ½ cup slivered cooked pork or chicken
> 1 green onion, sliced
> 2 ounces tofu, cubed
> 2 tablespoons lemon juice
> 1 tablespoon dry sherry
> ¼ teaspoon ground pepper
> 2 tablespoons cornstarch
> 2 tablespoons water
> 1 egg, slightly beaten
> ½ teaspoon sesame oil

1. Soak mushrooms in the boiling water 10 minutes. Drain and cut into slivers. Reserve.

2. In a 4-quart microwave-safe casserole, combine stock, soy sauce, pork, onion, and reserved mushrooms. Cover and microwave on high (100%) until boiling (8 to 10 minutes).

3. Add tofu, lemon juice, sherry, and pepper. Cover and microwave on high until boiling (1 to 3 minutes).

4. Stir together cornstarch and the 2 tablespoons water until smooth. Stir into soup. Microwave on high until slightly thickened and boiling (1½ to 2½ minutes). Remove from microwave and slowly pour in egg, stirring constantly. Stir in sesame oil. Ladle soup into bowls and serve hot.

Makes 4 cups, 4 servings.

CASSEROLES

Wholesome and nutritious, casseroles are the entrée you can count on to stay warm in the oven until family members on different schedules have eaten. And they make excellent leftovers that can be reheated for a quick bite.

CARROT-NUT LASAGNE ROLLS

Make these rolls and refrigerate them early in the day, then microwave them at dinnertime for an easy meal for your family.

      8 *lasagne noodles*
      1 *tablespoon olive oil*
      1 *cup grated carrots*
         (2 medium)
      1 *cup chopped walnuts*
      1 *medium onion, chopped*
      1 *clove garlic, minced*
      1 *teaspoon salt*
     ½ *teaspoon ground pepper*
     ½ *teaspoon Italian seasoning*
      1 *cup ricotta cheese*
      2 *cups spaghetti sauce*
      2 *tablespoons grated Parmesan cheese, for sprinkling*

1. Cook noodles conventionally, following package directions. Drain thoroughly.

2. In a 2-quart microwave-safe casserole, combine oil, carrots, walnuts, onion, and garlic. Cover and microwave on high (100%) until onions are tender (4 to 5 minutes). Add salt, pepper, and Italian seasoning. Stir in ricotta cheese.

3. Cover the bottom of a shallow 2-quart microwave-safe baking dish with ½ cup of the spaghetti sauce. Place noodles on a flat surface and spread ¼ cup cheese mixture on each noodle. Roll up noodle, starting at narrow end, and place rolled noodle on top of spaghetti sauce in dish, seam side down. Repeat with remaining noodles and cover with remaining 1½ cups sauce.

4. Cover dish and microwave on high 3 to 4 minutes. Spoon sauce from bottom of dish over rolled noodles and microwave, covered, on high until lasagne is hot (2 to 3 minutes). Sprinkle with Parmesan cheese and let lasagne stand, covered, 10 minutes before serving.

Serves 4.

Add an international touch to almost any meal with tart Greek Avgolemono, its lemon flavor underscored by crescents of fresh lemon floating on the soup.

Creamy soft cabbage leaves enfold a flavorful combination of cheeses and vegetables in this winning vegetarian entrée.

VEGETABLE-STUFFED CABBAGE ROLLS

The surprise in these stuffed cabbage rolls is the untraditional vegetable and cheese filling. A different twist on an old favorite, this eye-appealing dish could easily play the starring role in a vegetarian dinner.

    1 medium head cabbage
    1 tablespoon butter or
       margarine
    1½ cups broccoli florets
    1 cup sliced fresh mushrooms
    ⅓ cup thinly sliced carrots
    1 small onion, chopped
    1 small zucchini, chopped
    1 clove garlic, minced
    ½ teaspoon dried basil
    1 package (8 oz) cream cheese,
       at room temperature
    1 egg
    1 cup shredded Cheddar cheese
    1 cup tomato sauce
    2 tablespoons water

1. Rinse cabbage and wrap loosely in waxed paper. Microwave on high (100%) until outer leaves are soft (4 to 6 minutes), turning over halfway through cooking time. Remove and reserve 8 leaves, saving the rest for another use; let cool.

2. In a 2-quart microwave-safe casserole, combine butter, broccoli, mushrooms, carrots, onion, zucchini, garlic, and basil. Cover mixture and microwave on high until vegetables are crisp-tender (3 to 5 minutes). Let cool.

3. Combine cream cheese, egg, and Cheddar cheese with cooled vegetables. Place 2 tablespoons of the vegetable-cheese mixture in center of each of the 8 cooled cabbage leaves; roll, tucking in ends of leaf.

4. In an 8- by 12-inch microwave-safe baking dish, arrange cabbage rolls seam side down. Combine tomato sauce and the water. Pour over cabbage rolls. Cover and microwave on high until cabbage is tender (12 to 14 minutes), spooning sauce over cabbage rolls as they cook. Let stand, covered, 10 minutes. To serve, spoon sauce over each cabbage roll.

Serves 4.

FOUR-BEAN CASSEROLE BAKE

An interesting variation of baked beans, this casserole will be a hit when served with burgers at your next barbecue. With your microwave and this recipe, there is no reason to heat up your kitchen on a hot day. You can prepare the beans ahead through step 2; if you do, refrigerate them and add 2 to 3 minutes to the microwave cooking time given in the final step.

    8 slices bacon, cut into
       1-inch-long pieces
    1 medium onion, chopped
    ⅓ cup firmly packed brown
       sugar
    1 teaspoon dry mustard
    ¼ teaspoon garlic salt
    2 cups cooked green beans,
       drained
    1 can (16 oz) pork and beans,
       drained
    1 can (16 oz) kidney beans,
       drained
    1 can (16 oz) butter beans,
       drained

1. In a 4-quart microwave-safe casserole, combine bacon pieces and onion. Microwave on high (100%) until onion is soft and bacon begins to brown (5 to 7 minutes).

2. Stir in brown sugar, mustard, and garlic salt. Microwave on high until mixture boils and sugar is dissolved (2 to 3 minutes). Add all beans, stirring to combine.

3. Cover and microwave on high until hot (4 to 6 minutes). Let stand, covered, 5 minutes. Stir and serve.

Serves 8.

... FOR CASSEROLES

Casseroles and microwave ovens make a great team. These tips will ensure success.

☐ Ingredients in the same casserole should have similar microwave cooking times.

☐ Place faster-cooking foods on the bottom of a casserole dish; for example, rice should be placed under meat. The microwaves will take longer to reach the faster-cooking rice.

☐ Casseroles whose ingredients can be stirred cook most evenly.

☐ Use medium (50%) power and a longer cooking time for layered casseroles such as lasagne, which cannot be stirred, so that the center of the casserole heats without the outer edges overcooking.

☐ Add toppings such as cheese, bread crumbs, or onion rings at the end of the cooking time. The toppings will be warmed by the heat from the food.

☐ When preparing casseroles to freeze and reheat, omit toppings until after reheating.

☐ Cut vegetables and meats to be used in a casserole into similar sizes and shapes for even cooking.

☐ Cover casseroles during cooking to retain heat and prevent splatters.

☐ Allow casseroles to stand, covered, at least 10 minutes after cooking. Extra moisture will be absorbed and serving will be easier.

A confetti-like sprinkling of chopped carrot, green onion, and mushrooms makes Vegetable Pilaf a colorful side dish, appropriate for many meals.

VEGETABLE PILAF

This attractive, colorful pilaf is delicious served with chicken, turkey, or veal dishes.

    1 cup uncooked rice
    2 cups hot water
    2 tablespoons butter or
       margarine
    1 medium carrot, chopped
    ½ cup sliced green onion
    1 clove garlic, minced
    1 cup sliced fresh mushrooms
    2 teaspoons chicken bouillon
       Salt and freshly ground
       pepper, to taste
       Chopped parsley, for garnish

1. In a 3-quart microwave-safe casserole, combine rice, the hot water, and butter. Cover and microwave on high (100%) until rice has boiled 5 minutes (12 to 15 minutes total).

2. Add carrot, green onion, garlic, mushrooms, and bouillon. Cover and microwave on high until rice and vegetables are tender and water is absorbed (6 to 8 minutes).

3. Fluff rice with a fork. Season with salt and pepper and garnish with chopped parsley.

Serves 4.

PASTITSIO

This popular Greek casserole has several steps of preparation, but it can be assembled ahead to freeze or refrigerate until needed. It is a simple family dish that is also elegant enough for a buffet dinner for guests. It can be served hot or at room temperature.

- 1 pound ground beef
- 1 medium onion, finely chopped
- ½ teaspoon salt
- ¼ teaspoon freshly ground pepper
- ¼ teaspoon ground cinnamon
- 1 package (8 oz) ziti
- 1 egg, beaten
- ¼ cup butter or margarine
- 2 tablespoons flour
- ½ teaspoon salt
- 1 cup milk
- 1 egg, slightly beaten
- 2 tablespoons grated Parmesan cheese, for sprinkling
- ½ teaspoon paprika, for sprinkling

1. In a 1½-quart microwave-safe casserole, combine beef, onion, salt, pepper, and cinnamon. Microwave on high (100%) until beef is browned and onion is tender (4 to 6 minutes). Drain well and reserve.

2. Meanwhile, cook ziti conventionally, according to package directions. Drain well, let cool until lukewarm, and stir in beaten egg.

3. To prepare sauce, in a 2-cup microwave-safe measure, microwave butter on high until melted (30 to 60 seconds). Stir in flour and salt until smooth. Gradually stir in milk. Microwave on high 1 minute. Stir. Microwave again on high until mixture is thickened (1 to 2½ minutes). Let cool slightly, then stir in slightly beaten egg.

4. To assemble casserole, in the bottom of a 3-quart microwave-safe baking dish, place half of cooked ziti. Top with all of meat mixture. Cover with remaining ziti. Pour sauce over top. Combine Parmesan cheese and paprika and sprinkle over casserole.

5. Microwave on medium-high (70%) until sauce is set and mixture is hot (4 to 6 minutes). Let casserole stand 15 minutes before serving.

Serves 4 to 6.

BAKED LENTILS

Nutritious lentils are often overlooked as a side dish because they require long, slow cooking. Here is a recipe that allows you to prepare delicious lentils in about 20 minutes.

- 1 cup dried lentils
- 2 cups hot water
- 2 tablespoons vegetable oil
- 1 cup chopped onion
- 2 cloves garlic, minced
- 1 cup chopped green bell pepper (1 large)
- 2 cups crushed tomatoes, drained
- 1 teaspoon chili powder
- ½ teaspoon ground cumin
- ½ teaspoon salt
- ¼ teaspoon ground pepper
- ½ cup chopped black olives, for topping

1. In a 2-quart microwave-safe casserole, combine lentils and the water. Cover and microwave on high (100%) until lentils are tender (6 to 8 minutes), stirring twice during cooking time. Set aside.

2. In a 3-quart microwave-safe casserole, microwave oil on high until hot (1 to 2 minutes). Add onion, garlic, and bell pepper. Microwave on high until onion and bell pepper are tender (3 to 5 minutes). Stir in tomatoes, chili powder, cumin, salt, and ground pepper.

3. Drain reserved lentils and add to tomato mixture. Smooth top of lentil-tomato mixture and sprinkle with chopped olives. Cover and microwave on high until mixture is hot (3 to 5 minutes). Let stand, covered, 10 minutes before serving.

Serves 4.

VEGETARIAN DINNER

Mushroom-Cheese Dip

Assorted Crisp Crackers

Spinach-Stuffed Shells

Cherry Tomato Ratatouille

Tossed Green Salad

Sherried Fruit Compote

Orange-Mint Iced Tea (see page 30)

Vegetables appear in many dishes, from appetizers to desserts. Rich in vitamins and low in fat, they are excellent choices for a nutritious, versatile meal. Invite your friends to share a vegetarian dinner for four to six (with enough dessert for leftovers) and surprise them with this variety of dishes. Serve the mushroom appetizer with a selection of crisp crackers. The main course—colorful stuffed shells and ratatouille—will look delicious on your best plain white china. Accompany the meal with a tossed salad of the freshest greens and end with a light fruit compote for dessert.

MUSHROOM-CHEESE DIP

This dip is attractive served at room temperature in a small hollowed-out eggplant.

- *2 tablespoons sesame oil*
- *1 cup sliced fresh mushrooms*
- *½ cup thinly sliced green onions, including green tops*
- *1 clove garlic, minced*
- *1 package (8 oz) cream cheese*
- *1 jar (5 oz) sharp, pasteurized, processed cheese spread (see Note)*
- *¼ teaspoon ground pepper*
- *¼ cup sour cream*
- *Assorted crisp crackers, for accompaniment*

1. In a 1-quart microwave-safe casserole, microwave oil on high (100%) until hot (2 to 3 minutes). Add mushrooms, green onion, and garlic. Microwave on high until green onion is soft (2 to 3 minutes).

2. Add cream cheese and cheese spread and microwave on medium (50%) until cheeses are soft (3 to 5 minutes). Add pepper and sour cream and stir until mixture is thoroughly blended. Serve with crackers.

Makes about 1½ cups.

Note Processed cheeses melt more evenly than hard or dry cheeses.

SPINACH-STUFFED SHELLS

These tasty stuffed shells freeze well, so prepare a double recipe and freeze half to serve another time, but be sure to microwave each package of creamed spinach individually to prevent overcooking.

- *12 ounces jumbo macaroni shells (about 20 shells)*
- *1 package (9 oz) frozen creamed spinach*
- *1 cup ricotta cheese*
- *1 cup grated mozzarella cheese*
- *½ teaspoon salt*
- *¼ teaspoon ground pepper*
- *¾ cup chopped walnuts*
- *2 cups spaghetti sauce*

1. Cook shells conventionally, following package directions. Drain thoroughly.

2. Remove plastic bag of spinach from box and slit bag on one flat surface. Place bag in a 2-quart microwave-safe bowl and microwave on high (100%) until hot (5 to 6 minutes). Turn spinach out of package into bowl. Let cool slightly. Stir in cheeses, salt, and pepper. Stuff each shell with 1 tablespoon spinach mixture. Arrange stuffed shells in a 2-quart microwave-safe baking dish and set aside.

3. In a medium bowl combine walnuts and spaghetti sauce. Microwave on high until hot (2 to 3 minutes).

4. Pour sauce over stuffed shells. Cover and microwave on high until shells and sauce are hot (6 to 8 minutes). Let dish stand, covered, 10 minutes.

Serves 4 to 6.

CHERRY TOMATO RATATOUILLE

Cutting cherry tomatoes in half will make them easier to eat and enhance the tomato flavor in this dish. The flavor develops during overnight refrigeration, making this an easy vegetable to prepare ahead. It is good served either cold or warm.

- *1½ cups peeled and sliced zucchini (1 medium)*
- *1½ cups peeled and cubed eggplant (½ small)*
- *1 large green pepper, chopped*
- *1 small red onion, thinly sliced*
- *2 tablespoons olive oil*
- *1½ cups cherry tomato halves*

1. In a 3-quart microwave-safe casserole, combine zucchini, eggplant, pepper, onion, and olive oil. Cover and microwave on high (100%) until vegetables are crisp-tender (4 to 6 minutes), stirring twice. Stir in cherry tomato halves, cover, and microwave on high until tomatoes are hot (1 to 2 minutes).

2. Refrigerate, covered, 4 to 6 hours or overnight to allow flavors to blend. Serve cold or reheat and serve warm. To reheat, microwave, covered, on high until warm but not hot (2 to 3 minutes).

Serves 4 to 6.

SHERRIED FRUIT COMPOTE

A fruit compote is an elegant, light dessert. Use your favorite fresh fruits, including strawberries, blueberries, apples, and oranges. If fresh fruit is not available, substitute one 16-ounce can of fruit for each 2 cups of fresh fruit specified in the recipe.

- *2 cups fresh pineapple chunks*
- *2 cups peeled and sliced fresh peaches (3 to 4 peaches)*
- *2 cups peeled and sliced fresh pears (about 2 pears)*
- *2 bananas, peeled and sliced*
- *1 jar (8 oz) whole maraschino cherries (about ½ cup)*
- *¼ cup butter or margarine*
- *½ cup sugar*
- *2 tablespoons cornstarch*
- *¾ cup cream sherry*

1. In a decorative 2-quart microwave-safe serving dish, combine pineapple, peaches, pears, bananas, and cherries. Set aside.

2. In a 2-cup microwave-safe measure, microwave butter on high (100%) until melted (30 to 60 seconds). Add sugar, cornstarch, and sherry; stir until smooth. Microwave on medium (50%) until mixture is thickened and boiling (3 to 5 minutes), stirring twice.

3. Pour sherry mixture over reserved fruit; microwave on high until warm (3 to 4 minutes), stirring once. Serve warm (or see Note).

Serves 8 to 10.

Note Leftovers may be stored in the refrigerator and served cold, or to reheat, microwave 30 to 60 seconds per cup of compote.

Serve Spinach-Stuffed Shells,
Cherry Tomato Ratatouille, and
a warm Sherried Fruit
Compote for a memorable
vegetarian dinner.

A variation on the usual cold presentation, this Hot Chicken Salad (see page 68) served with brown rice is a delightful light meal for a cool summer evening.

Easy and Elegant Entrées

S elect a variety of entrées from this chapter, including fish, poultry, beef, pork, or lamb. From Trout With Wild Rice Stuffing (see page 61) to Five-Spice Drumsticks (see page 70) and Sweet and Sour Beef (see page 76), these simple and elegant dishes are all prepared easily in the microwave. With a browning dish you can quickly sear the meat for tender, delicious Lemon-Mint Lamb Chops (see page 77) and Veal Parmesan (see page 79). Tips for cooking meats (see page 76) provide steps to success, allowing you to present tasty and elegant meals in a flash.

Stuff the day's catch of trout with wild rice in this stunning presentation that is sure to please.

SEAFOOD

Seafood is a perfect candidate for microwaving—it is moist and cooks quickly.

BAKED HERBED BLUEFISH

Bluefish is found off the East Coast and in the Gulf of Mexico; if it is not available in your local market, halibut and mahimahi are effective substitutes. If you grow herbs in your garden, use them in this dish. They will impart a delicious flavor during cooking and provide an attractive garnish when the fish is served.

> 4 *bluefish fillets (about 2 lb total)*
> 2 *tablespoons butter or margarine*
> ¼ *cup chopped fresh parsley or 1 teaspoon dried parsley*
> 1 *tablespoon fresh oregano or 1 teaspoon dried oregano*
> ½ *teaspoon freshly ground pepper*
> ⅓ *cup dry white wine*
> *Sprigs of fresh parsley and oregano, for garnish*
> *Lemon or lime slices, for garnish*

1. Rinse fish and pat dry; place in a 9-inch-square microwave-safe baking dish. Dot top of fish with butter and sprinkle with the chopped parsley and oregano and pepper.

2. Pour wine around fish, cover with waxed paper, and microwave on high (100%) until fish flakes easily with a fork (6 to 10 minutes). Garnish with herb sprigs and lemon slices. Serve immediately.

Serves 4.

FLOUNDER FLORENTINE

Spinach cooked in the microwave retains the characteristic rich green color, making the contrasting hues of this dish a feast for the eyes.

> 10 *ounces spinach (fresh or frozen), washed, chopped, cooked, and drained*
> ½ *cup sliced mushrooms*
> ½ *cup shredded mozzarella cheese*
> ¼ *teaspoon each salt and freshly ground pepper*
> 8 *small flounder fillets (about 1½ lb total)*
> ¼ *cup dry white wine Paprika, for sprinkling*

1. In a large bowl combine hot spinach, mushrooms, cheese, salt, and pepper. Stir until cheese is partially melted.

2. Lay fillets side by side on work surface. Place 2 tablespoons spinach mixture on each. Beginning at small end, roll each fillet and place seam side down in a 9-inch-square microwave-safe baking dish. Repeat with all fillets. Pour wine over fillets, cover with waxed paper, and microwave on high (100%) until fish is opaque and flakes easily with a fork (6 to 8 minutes). Let stand, covered, 5 minutes. Sprinkle fish with paprika and serve.

Serves 4.

GARLIC-BUTTERED SHRIMP

What could be quicker or easier for supper than this tasty shrimp dish? Serve it with a tossed green salad and lots of French bread.

> 4 tablespoons butter
> 6 large cloves garlic, minced
> 1 pound (about 4 dozen) medium-sized shrimp, peeled and deveined
> ½ teaspoon salt
> ¼ teaspoon freshly ground pepper
> Lemon wedges, for garnish

1. In a 2-quart microwave-safe casserole, microwave butter on medium (50%) until melted (2 to 3 minutes).

2. Add garlic and shrimp and microwave on high (100%) until shrimp are pink (3 to 4 minutes), stirring once during cooking.

3. Season with salt and pepper, garnish with lemon wedges, and serve immediately.

Serves 4.

TROUT WITH WILD RICE STUFFING

When the trout fisherman has a successful day, celebrate the catch with this elegant dish. The wild rice stuffing cooks quickly in the microwave.

> 1 package (6 oz) long-grain and wild rice
> 1 small onion, chopped
> ¼ cup chopped celery
> 4 small trout (1½ to 2 lb total), cleaned, heads and tails on
> 1 tablespoon butter, melted

1. Prepare rice according to microwave instructions on package. Stir in onion and celery.

2. Wash fish and dry cavities with paper towel. Fill cavities with rice. Place microwave rack in an 8- by 12-inch microwave-safe baking dish. Place stuffed fish on rack, allowing thin edges of fish to overlap slightly.

3. Brush fish with melted butter. Cover with waxed paper and microwave on high (100%) until fish flakes easily with a fork in thickest portion (10 to 13 minutes). Let stand, covered, 5 minutes.

Serves 4.

Serve Garlic-Buttered Shrimp, French bread to mop up the excess garlic butter, and a salad of the most elegant greens for an easy, attractive meal.

BAKED SCALLOPS

Prepare this recipe with tiny bay scallops or larger sea scallops, but remember that the sea scallops may require 30 to 60 seconds longer cooking. Begin this meal with Fresh Tomato Bisque (see page 49), serve the scallops on brown rice accompanied by fresh vegetable kabobs, and for dessert try an old-fashioned blueberry grunt.

    4 slices bacon
    2 tablespoons butter or
       margarine
    2 tablespoons flour
    1 cup milk
    1 teaspoon salt
    ½ teaspoon white pepper
    1 cup shredded Gruyère cheese
    1 pound bay scallops or sea
       scallops
    ¼ cup chopped pimiento
    1 tablespoon chopped chives

1. Place bacon slices on a paper towel–covered microwave-safe plate. Cover with another paper towel and microwave on high (100%) until bacon is crisp (2 to 3 minutes). Crumble and set aside.

2. In a 4-cup microwave-safe measure, microwave butter on high until melted (1 to 2 minutes). Stir in flour until mixture is smooth. Gradually stir in milk. Microwave on high 1 minute. Stir and microwave again on high until sauce thickens (1 to 1½ minutes). Remove from microwave and stir in salt, pepper, and cheese until cheese is melted.

3. In a 1½-quart microwave-safe baking dish, combine sauce, scallops, pimiento, and chives. Microwave on medium (50%) until scallops are hot (4 to 5 minutes), stirring once. Sprinkle with crumbled bacon and serve immediately.

Serves 4.

... FOR FISH

Fish is an ideal food for microwaving because it has a high moisture content. You will also appreciate the lack of a lingering fishy odor in your kitchen.

☐ Be careful not to overcook fish, since it cooks quickly. Test frequently and stop cooking just as the fish begins to flake. Some additional cooking will occur during standing time.

☐ Fish will change from translucent to opaque as it cooks.

☐ Cook fish on high (100%) unless you notice some popping. Occasionally, oily fish pop during microwaving since the fat in the flesh heats quickly. If this occurs, reduce the power to medium (50%) and check carefully for doneness.

☐ Always defrost frozen fish and allow temperature of fish to equalize before cooking. The delicate flesh will cook unevenly if you try to defrost and cook in one step.

☐ Real shells are safe to use in the microwave for heating individual servings of fish.

☐ To open shellfish in the microwave, on a microwave-safe plate microwave 3 or 4 shellfish at a time on high (100%) until shells just begin to open (20 to 45 seconds).

☐ Use medium (50%) power when reheating fish to prevent drying and overcooking.

☐ Cover fish during cooking unless fish is breaded. Any cover is satisfactory, but waxed paper retains steam and doesn't stick to fish.

☐ Shield head and tail of whole fish with strips of aluminum foil during cooking. Foil will direct microwave energy to fleshier portion of fish to ensure even cooking.

☐ Line baking dish with paper towels during cooking to absorb excess moisture from fish. Or if you prefer that fish not sit in its cooking liquid, place fish on microwave-safe rack so moisture will drain away.

☐ To enhance flavor and provide color, season fish as you would for conventional cooking—with butter, parsley, lemon juice, or wine.

MARINATED HALIBUT STEAKS

Use individual steaks or one large steak cut into four pieces. Marinate the fish at least 2 hours, but if you need to let it stand another 2 to 4 hours, it will be just as good.

  4 halibut steaks (about
     2 lb total)
  1 clove garlic, minced
  1 small onion, chopped
  ¼ cup chopped green bell pepper
  ½ teaspoon ground cumin
  ½ teaspoon ground thyme
  ¾ cup olive oil
  2 tablespoons lemon juice

1. Wash fish and pat dry with paper towel; place fish in an 8- by 12-inch microwave-safe baking dish.

2. To make marinade, in a 1-pint glass jar with lid, combine garlic, onion, bell pepper, cumin, thyme, oil, and lemon juice. Shake well. Pour marinade over fish. Cover and refrigerate at least 2 hours.

3. Remove fish from dish. Pour off oil from marinade, reserving pepper and onion. Place fish again in baking dish and cover with reserved bell pepper and onion. Cover with waxed paper and microwave on high (100%) until fish flakes easily with a fork (10 to 12 minutes). Serve immediately.

Serves 4.

Baked Scallops—in a light Gruyère cheese sauce flavored with pimiento and chives and topped with crumbled bacon—is delicious accompanied by brown rice and kabobs of your favorite fresh vegetables.

Fresh mussels in their shells sparkle in a colorful tomato and wine sauce in Mussels Italian Style— prepared simply and easily in the microwave.

BAKED FISH WITH VEGETABLES

Cucumber, carrot, and celery are combined to produce a flavorful baked fish that is ideal for calorie counters.

> 1 cucumber, peeled, seeded, and chopped
> 1 medium carrot, peeled and shredded
> 1 medium stalk celery, washed and chopped
> 1 clove garlic, minced
> ¼ cup chopped parsley
> 3 tablespoons lemon juice
> ½ teaspoon dill
> 4 sole or flounder fillets (about 1 lb total)

1. In a medium bowl combine cucumber, carrot, celery, garlic, parsley, lemon juice, and dill. Set aside.

2. Fold each fillet in half crosswise and place in a 9-inch-square microwave-safe baking dish, with folds to outside of dish. Spoon vegetable mixture over fillets.

3. Cover fish with waxed paper and microwave on high (100%) until fish flakes easily with a fork (5 to 7 minutes). Let fish stand, covered, 5 minutes.

Serves 4.

POACHED FILLETS
WITH CRACKED PEPPER

A hint of pepper gives this dish a unique flavor.

  6 to 8 whole peppercorns
  ½ cup dry white wine
  1 bay leaf
  1 tablespoon chopped celery
    leaves
  4 sole or flounder fillets
    (about 1 lb total)

1. Crack peppercorns by enclosing them in a dish towel and lightly tapping with a mallet or hammer. In a 2-cup microwave-safe measure, combine cracked peppercorns, wine, bay leaf, and celery leaves. Microwave on high (100%) until mixture is boiling (1 to 1½ minutes).

2. Fold each fillet in half crosswise and arrange fillets in a 9-inch-square microwave-safe baking dish, with folds to outside of dish. Pour hot wine mixture over fish. Cover with waxed paper.

3. Microwave on high until fish begins to flake with a fork (5 to 7 minutes). Let stand, covered, 5 minutes.

Serves 4.

HOT TUNA TACOS

Use water-packed tuna to produce a zesty light dinner that dieters will appreciate. Prepare it in less than 10 minutes in the microwave.

  1 can (6 oz) tuna
  1 small onion, chopped
  1 can (4 oz) jalapeño peppers,
    chopped
  ⅓ cup plain yogurt
  ½ teaspoon chili powder
  4 taco shells
  1 cup shredded Monterey
    jack cheese
  1 cup shredded iceberg lettuce
  2 medium tomatoes, washed,
    seeded, and chopped

1. In a 1½-quart microwave-safe casserole, combine tuna, onion, peppers, yogurt, and chili powder. Microwave on high (100%) until hot (2 to 3 minutes), stirring once.

2. Divide tuna mixture evenly among taco shells. Top with cheese and place on a microwave-safe plate. Microwave on high until cheese is melted (1 to 1½ minutes). Remove from microwave and top with lettuce and tomatoes. Serve immediately.

Serves 4.

MUSSELS ITALIAN STYLE

Mussels can be a special treat collected at a beach outing. Let the mussels soak in a bucket of seawater for a few hours so they can filter themselves and become less gritty. When you return home, scrub and debeard them. Preparation in the microwave is the answer to cooking this dish quickly on a hot summer evening.

  1 can (16 oz) stewed tomatoes
  1 can (6 oz) tomato paste
  1 small onion, chopped
  1 tablespoon chopped parsley
  ½ cup dry red wine
    Salt and freshly ground
    pepper, to taste
  2 pounds mussels in shells
    (24 to 28 mussels), scrubbed
    and debearded

1. In a 3-quart microwave-safe casserole, combine tomatoes, tomato paste, onion, parsley, and wine. Microwave on high (100%) until sauce begins to bubble (6 to 8 minutes). Season with salt and pepper.

2. Add mussels. Cover and microwave on high until shells begin to open (6 to 8 minutes), stirring twice. Let stand, covered, 5 minutes.

Serves 4.

menu

SUMMER SEASHORE
CELEBRATION

Chilled Mint Soup

Crabmeat-Stuffed Flounder

Steamed Snow Peas (see page 45)

*Sliced Garden Tomatoes
With Fresh Basil*

Glazed Strawberry Tart

Chenin Blanc

Celebrate the bounty of summer with fresh seafood and fruit and vegetables ripe from the garden. Include crisp snow peas, steamed quickly in the microwave, and vine-ripened tomatoes sprinkled with snipped fresh basil from the herb garden. Serve the refreshing chilled soup in small crystal bowls and float blossoms on each. The elegant strawberry tart, brimming with choice fruit and glistening with a jelly glaze, is the perfect finish to a warm summer evening under the stars. Serve this delightful meal for four (with enough dessert for second helpings) on the beach, by the pool, or on the patio.

CHILLED MINT SOUP

Pinch back the mint in your herb garden and use it in this refreshing soup. Then on the surface float rose petals, the colorful blossoms of such plants as nasturtiums or chives, or the delicate sky blue flowers of borage from the herb garden.

> 2 tablespoons butter or margarine
> ¼ cup thinly sliced green onion
> 2 tablespoons flour
> 1 cup chicken stock
> ½ cup packed mint leaves
> 1 tablespoon chopped parsley
> 1 cup half-and-half
> Flower blossoms or rose petals, for garnish

1. In a 4-cup microwave-safe measure, microwave butter on high (100%) until melted (30 to 60 seconds). Stir in green onion and microwave on high until onion is soft (1 to 2 minutes). Stir in flour until mixture is well blended. Gradually stir in stock. Microwave on high 1 minute. Stir, then microwave again on high until mixture is thickened (1 to 2½ minutes). Stir in mint and parsley.

2. Pour mixture into work bowl of food processor. Process until mixture is puréed (10 to 15 seconds), scraping down bowl once. With processor running, slowly pour in half-and-half until mixture is well blended. Cover and place in refrigerator at least 3 hours, or until thoroughly chilled.

3. To serve, ladle soup into small crystal bowls and float a blossom on the surface of each.

Makes 3 cups, 4 servings.

CRABMEAT-STUFFED FLOUNDER

This popular dish, often found on restaurant menus, is easy to prepare at home.

> 4 tablespoons butter or margarine
> 2 green onions (including tops), minced
> 4 tablespoons flour
> 1 cup milk
> ¾ teaspoon dry mustard
> ½ cup grated Swiss cheese
> ¼ cup dried bread crumbs
> ½ teaspoon salt
> ¼ teaspoon freshly ground pepper
> ½ pound crabmeat, cut into small chunks
> 8 small flounder fillets (1½ to 2 lb total)
> Paprika, for sprinkling
> Lemon wedges, for garnish

1. In a 4-cup microwave-safe measure, combine butter and green onion. Microwave on high (100%) until butter is melted and green onion is tender (1½ to 2½ minutes), stirring once.

2. Stir in flour until mixture is smooth. Gradually stir in milk. Microwave on high 1 minute. Stir and microwave again on high until mixture boils and thickens (1 to 2½ minutes), stirring once during cooking.

3. Add mustard and cheese; stir until cheese is melted. Stir in bread crumbs, salt, pepper, and crabmeat.

4. In an 8- by 12-inch microwave-safe baking dish, lay 4 of the fillets. Divide filling evenly among them, spreading to cover each fillet. Use remaining 4 fillets to top each covered fillet (see Note). Sprinkle with paprika and cover with waxed paper.

5. Microwave on high until fish is opaque and flakes easily with a fork (6 to 8 minutes). Garnish with lemon wedges and serve immediately.

Serves 4.

Note Individual fillets can also be spread with filling and rolled, to make 8 rolls.

GLAZED STRAWBERRY TART

Select the freshest, most perfectly shaped berries since they are the stars of this gorgeous dessert.

> 1 package (8 oz) cream cheese
> ½ cup confectioners' sugar
> 1 tablespoon milk
> 1 quart strawberries, washed and hulled

Flaky Pastry

> ¼ cup butter or margarine, softened (see page 87)
> ⅓ cup confectioners' sugar
> 1¼ cups flour

Jelly Glaze

> 1 jar (10 oz) strawberry jelly
> 2 tablespoons lemon juice

1. Prepare Flaky Pastry and Jelly Glaze; set both aside to cool. In a medium microwave-safe mixing bowl, microwave cream cheese on medium (50%) until softened (1 to 2 minutes). Add sugar and milk, stirring until smooth.

2. Pour filling into cooled Flaky Pastry, spreading evenly. Arrange strawberries in decorative pattern on top, with pointed ends up. Spoon cooled Jelly Glaze evenly over berries. Refrigerate 3 to 4 hours.

Serves 8 to 10.

Flaky Pastry In a medium mixing bowl, combine butter, confectioners' sugar, and flour until butter is well mixed and crumbs are very fine. Press dough evenly into bottom and up sides of a lightly greased 10-inch-diameter microwave-safe quiche dish or pie plate. Microwave on high (100%) until surface appears dry (3 to 4½ minutes). Remove to wire rack to cool.

Makes one 10-inch pie crust.

Jelly Glaze In a 2-cup microwave-safe measure, combine jelly and lemon juice. Microwave on high until jelly is melted (1 to 2 minutes), stirring twice. Let cool 5 minutes.

Makes about 1¼ cups.

Nestle the stuffed flounder on snow peas, float fresh violets on the mint soup, and serve a gorgeous strawberry tart for an elegant summer meal.

The crunchy nut coating on this Southern Pecan Chicken confirms the regional origin of this elegant entrée. Garnish the chicken with fresh rosemary and toasted pecans.

POULTRY

Virtually every cooking method can be applied to poultry, but microwaving is surely the fastest. You may also be surprised by the moist succulence of poultry prepared in the microwave. See the chart on page 73 for poultry cooking times.

HOT CHICKEN SALAD

Most people think of chicken salad as a cold dish for a summer picnic. However, served hot, chicken salad can be just as delightful for dinner on a cool evening. Accompany it with brown rice, steamed broccoli, sliced oranges, and white Zinfandel.

    1 medium carrot, shredded
    ¼ cup chopped green bell pepper
    ¼ cup sliced green onion, plus
       green onion curls for garnish
    2 large whole chicken breasts
    ½ cup plain yogurt
    ¼ cup mayonnaise
    ½ teaspoon dried basil
       Salt, to taste

1. In a 2-cup microwave-safe measure, combine carrot, pepper, and sliced green onion. Microwave on high (100%) until pepper is crisptender (1 to 2 minutes). Set aside.

2. Wash chicken and pat dry with paper towels. Cut into bite-sized chunks and place in a 2-quart microwave-safe casserole. Cover with waxed paper and microwave on high until chicken is tender (4 to 6 minutes), stirring twice. Let chicken stand, covered, 5 minutes. Drain thoroughly.

3. In a 1-cup microwave-safe measure, combine yogurt, mayonnaise, basil, and salt. Microwave mixture on medium (50%) until hot (2 to 3 minutes).

4. To drained chicken chunks add reserved vegetables. Pour in yogurt mixture and toss to coat. Garnish with green onion curls and serve immediately.

Serves 4.

COQ AU VIN

This classic French chicken dish can now be cooked in record time with a microwave version of the recipe. It is still the main attraction of a country French dinner served with rice, a crisp green salad, crusty French bread, and a hearty red wine.

- ½ pound small white onions, peeled
- 2 tablespoons water
- 2 slices bacon
- 1 chicken (2½ to 3 lb), cut up
- ½ teaspoon salt
- ¼ teaspoon freshly ground pepper
- ¼ teaspoon ground thyme
- 1 bay leaf
- 1 clove garlic, minced
- 1 cup dry red table wine
- ½ cup chicken stock
- 1 cup sliced mushrooms

1. To a 1-quart microwave-safe casserole, add onions and the water. Cover and microwave on high (100%) until onions are crisp-tender when pierced with a fork (3½ to 5 minutes). Set aside.

2. Place bacon slices on a paper towel. Cover with another paper towel and microwave on high until bacon is crisp (2 to 3 minutes). Crumble and set aside.

3. Wash chicken pieces and pat dry with paper towels. Arrange in a deep 4-quart microwave-safe casserole. Add salt, pepper, thyme, bay leaf, garlic, wine, and stock. Cover with waxed paper and microwave on high until chicken is tender when pierced with a fork (15 to 20 minutes), rearranging pieces halfway through cooking time.

4. Stir in reserved onions and crumbled bacon. Add mushrooms. Cover and microwave on high until onions and mushrooms are hot (2 to 3 minutes). Let stand, covered, 10 minutes.

Serves 4.

SOUTHERN PECAN CHICKEN

Pecans grow in the southern states, where they are used in many dishes. Luckily pecans are widely available, and we can all enjoy this crunchy chicken dish. In honor of the southern heritage, serve this chicken with baked sweet potatoes, fresh green peas, and Georgia peach cobbler.

- ¾ cup pecan halves
- 2 tablespoons butter
- ½ cup flour
- 2 teaspoons paprika
- ½ teaspoon salt
- ¼ teaspoon freshly ground pepper
- ½ teaspoon dried rosemary
- ½ cup milk
- 4 whole chicken breasts, skinned, boned, split, and washed

1. To a 9-inch-square microwave-safe baking dish, add pecans and butter. Microwave on high (100%) until pecans are toasted (1 to 3 minutes), stirring twice. Reserve 2 tablespoons toasted pecans for garnish and set aside buttered dish for cooking chicken.

2. Chop remaining pecans and place in a shallow pie plate. Add flour, paprika, salt, pepper, and rosemary, stirring to blend.

3. Pour milk into a shallow bowl. Dip chicken in milk and then in pecan mixture, coating well. Place in buttered dish and cover with waxed paper. Microwave on medium-high (70%) until juices run clear when chicken is pierced with a fork (12 to 15 minutes). Garnish with reserved toasted pecans and let stand, covered, 5 minutes before serving.

Serves 4.

MICROWAVE GRAVY

Microwave gravy is the ultimate in convenience. Collect drippings during cooking. With a minimum of stirring or pot watching you will have hot, lump-free gravy.

1. *Pour drippings into a 4-cup microwave-safe measure. Let stand so fat can rise to surface; then skim fat from drippings.*

2. *Microwave skimmed drippings on high (100%) until boiling (1 to 4 minutes; time depends on amount of drippings). Meanwhile, in a small bowl combine thickener (flour, cornstarch, or arrowroot) and liquid (water, milk, or stock), allowing 1 tablespoon of thickener and 1 tablespoon of liquid for each cup of drippings. Rapidly stir thickened liquid into hot drippings, mixing well. Microwave on high until gravy boils and thickens (1 to 3 minutes), stirring every minute. Season to taste with salt and freshly ground pepper, and serve.*

... FOR POULTRY

Using these suggestions will convince you to microwave all the poultry you cook.

☐ When cooking a whole bird, begin with the breast side down for one third of the cooking time. Turn over and finish breast side up.

☐ Arrange chicken pieces with meatiest portions to the outside of the dish for even cooking.

☐ When roasting a bird, use wooden skewers to hold the wings and legs of the bird close to the body. The skewers are handy holders when you need to turn the bird over during cooking.

☐ Before and during roasting, baste the bird with melted butter or sherry for crisp, browned skin.

☐ Reduce oven spattering during cooking by covering food with a tent of waxed paper.

☐ Remove juices as they accumulate so that the microwaves cook the poultry efficiently rather than heating the juices.

☐ Use a microwave thermometer or an instant-read thermometer to check the temperature of the cooked poultry. Insert thermometer in thick portion of breast near thigh, without touching the bone. Cooked poultry should register a temperature of 175° F at completion of standing time.

☐ Let poultry stand, covered, at least 10 minutes for temperatures to equalize before carving and serving.

☐ If tips of wings or drumsticks begin to overcook, cover them with aluminum foil.

FIVE-SPICE DRUMSTICKS

Five-spice powder is slightly sweet—similar to a combination of cinnamon, cloves, and nutmeg—and has a delicious aroma. Look for it in the ethnic food section of your supermarket or an Asian grocery store.

6 to 8 chicken drumsticks
¾ teaspoon Chinese five-spice powder
½ teaspoon salt
½ teaspoon freshly ground pepper

1. Wash drumsticks and pat dry. Remove skin, if desired. For an authentic Asian presentation, loosen meat from thin end of each drumstick and pull meat down to form ball at large end.

2. In a small bowl combine five-spice powder, salt, and pepper. Rub over all surfaces of each drumstick.

3. In a 9- by 12-inch microwave-safe baking dish, arrange coated drumsticks, alternating thickest portions to outside of dish. Cover with waxed paper and microwave on high (100%) until juices run clear when drumsticks are pierced with a fork in meatiest portion (9 to 12 minutes). Let stand, covered, 5 minutes.

Serves 4.

ASIAN CHICKEN BAKE

Marinating the chicken for at least an hour produces a tasty Asian-style dish. Be sure to pass the hot marinade to spoon over the chicken. Serve it with rice and a fresh fruit salad with sesame dressing.

1 chicken (2½ to 3 lb), cut up
½ teaspoon garlic salt
½ teaspoon paprika
¾ cup soy sauce
½ cup vegetable oil
1 tablespoon rice vinegar or distilled white vinegar
1 teaspoon sugar
1 slice fresh ginger, minced
¼ teaspoon freshly ground pepper

1. Wash chicken pieces and pat dry with paper towels. Place pieces in an 8- by 12-inch microwave-safe baking dish, with meatier portions to outside of dish. Sprinkle with garlic salt and paprika.

2. In a 1-pint jar with lid, combine soy sauce, oil, vinegar, sugar, ginger, and pepper. Shake well to blend. Pour over chicken. Cover and let marinate in refrigerator at least 1 hour.

3. Remove from refrigerator. Spoon marinade in bottom of baking dish over chicken. Cover with waxed paper and microwave on high (100%) 10 minutes. Turn chicken pieces over and rearrange outside pieces to center of dish. Again spoon marinade over chicken. Cover and microwave on high, basting several times with marinade, until chicken is tender and juices are clear when chicken is pierced with a fork (8 to 10 minutes). Let stand, covered, 5 minutes.

Serves 4.

TURKEY MEATBALLS

With ground turkey increasingly available in supermarkets, it is easy to reduce the fat content of many dishes. Serve these meatballs with spaghetti and your favorite sauce for a healthy family dinner.

1 pound ground turkey
1 egg, beaten
1 medium onion, chopped
1 clove garlic, minced
½ cup dried bread crumbs
½ teaspoon salt
¼ teaspoon freshly ground pepper
¼ teaspoon dried oregano

1. In a medium bowl combine all ingredients. Mix lightly. Shape into about 16 large meatballs.

2. In a 9-inch-square microwave-safe baking dish, arrange meatballs in a single layer. Microwave on high (100%) until no longer pink (8 to 10 minutes), turning meatballs over once and moving meatballs in center to outside edge. Cover with waxed paper and let stand 5 minutes.

Serves 4.

Basting the chicken with a ginger-soy marinade gives this Asian Chicken Bake its glistening and delicious glaze.

The traditional French pairing of tarragon and chicken produces this memorable entrée. Sautéed sugar snap peas are the perfect accompaniment.

TURKEY STROGANOFF

Make this dish with leftover roast turkey or turkey cutlets that have been microwaved 3 to 4 minutes.

  2 tablespoons butter or
    margarine
  ½ cup chopped onion
  2 tablespoons flour
  ½ cup milk
  ½ cup chicken stock
  ½ teaspoon salt
  ¼ teaspoon freshly ground
    pepper
  ¼ teaspoon dried thyme
  2 cups cubed cooked turkey
  1 cup sliced mushrooms
  ½ cup sour cream

1. In a 4-cup microwave-safe measure, microwave butter on high (100%) until melted (30 to 60 seconds). Add onion and microwave on high until onion is soft (1 to 2½ minutes). Stir in flour until mixture is smooth. Stir in milk and stock. Microwave on high 1 minute. Stir and microwave again on high until thickened (1 to 2½ minutes), stirring twice. Stir in salt, pepper, and thyme.

2. Add turkey and mushrooms. Microwave on high until turkey is hot (2 to 3 minutes). Stir in sour cream and serve immediately.

Serves 4.

TERIYAKI CHICKEN KABOBS

You may want to double the marinade ingredients and store extra for future meals; the marinade will keep refrigerated for several weeks. Marinate the chicken cubes in the refrigerator overnight for a nutritious meal that is easy to fix when you are short of time.

- ½ cup soy sauce
- 1 clove garlic, crushed
- ½ teaspoon dry mustard
- 1 slice fresh ginger, minced
- 1 whole boneless chicken breast
- 1 small green bell pepper, seeded and cut into 1-inch cubes
- 4 small white onions, peeled
- 8 whole mushrooms
- 4 cherry tomatoes

1. In a 1-pint jar with lid, combine soy sauce, garlic, mustard, and ginger. Shake well to blend.

2. Wash chicken and pat dry with paper towels. Cut chicken into 1-inch cubes. Place in a sealable plastic bag and pour in marinade. Place bag in a bowl and refrigerate at least 2 hours, or overnight.

3. Remove chicken cubes from bag and pour marinade into a small bowl. On wooden or plastic microwave-safe skewers, alternate marinated chicken cubes with bell pepper, onions, and mushrooms.

4. Place microwave rack in a 9-inch-square microwave-safe baking dish. Lay kabobs on rack and brush with marinade. Cover with waxed paper and microwave on high (100%) until chicken is partially cooked (3 to 4 minutes). Turn kabobs over. Thread 1 cherry tomato on the tip of each skewer; brush kabobs with marinade. Cover and microwave on high until chicken is opaque and tender when pierced with a fork (2 to 3 minutes). Let stand, covered, 5 minutes.

Serves 4.

POULTRY ROASTING GUIDE

Poultry	Power Level	Cooking Time Per Pound
Chicken (under 3 lb)	High (100%)	6 to 9 minutes
Chicken (over 3 lb)	Medium (50%)	10 to 13 minutes
Turkey (up to 15 lb)	Medium (50%)	12 to 15 minutes
Duck	Medium (50%)	7 to 10 minutes
Cornish game hen	High (100%)	6½ to 8½ minutes

CHICKEN TARRAGON

Tarragon, a favorite herb in French cooking, makes this presentation special. Note that the chicken is browned in a microwave browning dish (see page 13). Accompany the chicken with sautéed sugar snap peas.

- 1 tablespoon butter or margarine
- 2 whole chicken breasts, halved, boned, skinned, washed, and dried
- ½ cup apple juice
- 3 tablespoons chopped fresh tarragon or 1½ teaspoons dried tarragon
- ½ teaspoon salt
- ¼ teaspoon paprika

1. Preheat a microwave browning dish in the microwave on high (100%) until hot (4 to 5 minutes). Add butter and stir to coat bottom of dish. Add chicken and microwave on high until lightly browned (1 to 1½ minutes). Turn chicken over and microwave on high until opaque (4 to 4½ minutes).

2. In a small bowl combine apple juice, tarragon, salt, and paprika. Pour over chicken. Microwave on high until chicken is tender (2 to 4 minutes). Cover chicken with waxed paper and let stand 5 minutes before serving.

Serves 4.

ORANGE CHICKEN

Although Chinese and Mexican cuisines are among those using oranges as a flavoring for poultry, this version is a simple but flavorful USA-inspired dish.

- 2 tablespoons butter or margarine
- 1 tablespoon cornstarch
- 1 cup freshly squeezed orange juice
- 1 teaspoon grated orange rind
- 1 chicken (2½ to 3 lb), cut up
  Fresh orange slices, for garnish

1. In a 2-cup microwave-safe measure, microwave butter on high (100%) until melted (30 to 60 seconds). Stir in cornstarch until mixture is smooth. Stir in orange juice gradually to prevent curdling. Microwave on high 1 minute. Stir and microwave again on high until thickened (1 to 2½ minutes). Stir in orange rind. Set aside.

2. Wash chicken pieces and pat dry with paper towels. In an 8- by 12-inch microwave-safe baking dish, arrange chicken pieces, with meatier portions to outside of dish. Pour orange sauce over chicken. Cover with waxed paper and microwave on high until chicken is tender (12 to 15 minutes), turning chicken pieces over once and basting several times with orange sauce. Let stand, covered, 10 minutes. Garnish with orange slices and serve.

Serves 4.

EASY STUFFINGS

For many people, stuffing is the main reason for cooking turkey or chicken. Stuffed poultry can be cooked in the microwave, but you will find the cooking time approximately double the time required to cook an un-stuffed bird. Stuffings, by themselves, heat quickly in the microwave and can be cooked while the bird is carved. If your family thinks stuffing is found only inside the bird, spoon the hot stuffing into the cavity before serving!

Allow 1 cup of stuffing per pound of bird.

BASIC STUFFING

 1 large onion, finely chopped
 ½ cup butter or margarine
 8 cups bread crumbs
 1 teaspoon freshly ground pepper

1. In a large microwave-safe bowl, combine onion and butter. Microwave on high (100%) until onion is soft (2 to 3 minutes).

2. Add bread crumbs and pepper. Toss lightly.

3. Stuff cooked bird or spoon lightly into a 3-quart microwave-safe casserole, cover, and microwave on high until hot (1 to 1½ minutes per cup of stuffing).

Makes 8 cups.

PORK-SAUSAGE STUFFING

Wonderful with either turkey or chicken, this is a Thanksgiving favorite.

 ½ pound pork sausage
 1 recipe Basic Stuffing (see above)
 ¾ teaspoon ground sage

In a 1-quart microwave-safe casserole, place pork sausage. Microwave on high (100%) until no pink remains (3 to 5 minutes). Drain and add to Basic Stuffing; add sage. Microwave as in step 3 of Basic Stuffing.

Makes 8 to 9 cups.

APPLE-AND-RAISIN STUFFING

The fruits give this stuffing a slightly sweet taste that complements fowl.

 1 recipe Basic Stuffing (see left)
 2 cups chopped apples (2 to 3 medium apples)
 ½ cup raisins
 1 teaspoon salt
 ½ teaspoon ground thyme

In a 3-quart microwave-safe bowl, place Basic Stuffing; add apples, raisins, salt, and thyme. Microwave as in step 3 of Basic Stuffing.

Makes about 10 cups.

SOUTHWESTERN CORN BREAD STUFFING

For a different twist try a stuffing with Mexican flavor. Bake the corn bread a day ahead and let it stand at room temperature so that it will be a little stale. South-of-the-Border Corn Bread makes a great stuffing base.

 1 large onion
 ½ cup butter or margarine
 1 teaspoon salt
 ½ teaspoon ground cumin
 1 teaspoon freshly ground pepper
 1 recipe South-of-the-Border Corn Bread (see page 33)

1. In a 2-quart microwave-safe bowl, combine onion and butter. Microwave on high (100%) until onion is soft (2 to 3 minutes). Stir in salt, cumin, and pepper.

2. Crumble South-of-the-Border Corn Bread and add to onion mixture, tossing lightly to blend. Microwave on high until hot (1 to 1½ minutes per cup of stuffing).

Makes 6 cups.

ROAST CHICKEN WITH SHERRY

Basting chicken with sherry as it roasts gives it a golden color and moist interior. Serve the roast chicken with buttered noodles and a spinach salad for an elegant, easy dinner.

 1 whole chicken (2½ to 3 lb)
 1 small onion, chopped
 1 tablespoon chopped parsley
 ¼ teaspoon salt
 ¼ cup sherry

1. Wash chicken inside and out and pat dry with paper towels. Combine onion, parsley, and salt; rub inside chicken. Tuck wings of chicken behind back and tie legs together with kitchen twine.

2. Place a microwave rack in an 8- by 12-inch microwave-safe baking dish. Place trussed chicken, breast side down, on rack, cover with waxed paper, and microwave on high (100%) 10 minutes, basting once with some of the sherry.

3. Turn chicken so breast side is up and baste again with sherry. Cover with waxed paper and microwave on high, basting with sherry several times, until juices run clear when thigh is pierced with a fork and drumstick moves easily (11 to 14 minutes). Let stand, covered, 10 minutes. If you desire a crispier skin, after the standing time place the chicken in a 400° F oven for 5 to 15 minutes.

Serves 4.

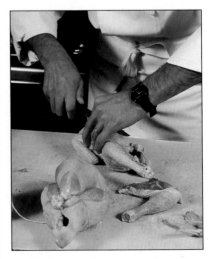

MEAT

Try cooking your favorite meats in the microwave oven. You will be delighted with the time you save when preparing dinner. See the chart on page 77 for suggested cooking times for beef, pork, lamb, and veal.

HAM LOAF WITH CREAMY MUSTARD SAUCE

The tangy mustard sauce is a perfect accompaniment to this ham loaf, a simple dish that is elegant enough for a special occasion.

- ¾ pound ground smoked ham
- ½ pound ground pork
- 1 egg, beaten
- 1 medium onion, chopped
- ¾ cup saltine cracker crumbs (about 16 crackers)
- ¼ teaspoon freshly ground pepper
- ¼ teaspoon ground cloves
- 1 tablespoon chopped parsley, for garnish

Creamy Mustard Sauce

- ½ cup sour cream or plain yogurt
- ¼ cup Dijon mustard

1. In a large bowl combine ham, pork, egg, onion, cracker crumbs, pepper, and cloves. Mix lightly.

2. Gather mixture into a loaf shape and place in a 9- by 5-inch microwave-safe loaf dish. Microwave on high (100%) until loaf is warm (5 minutes). Reduce power to medium (50%) and microwave until loaf is lightly browned and microwave thermometer registers 170° F (12 to 15 minutes). Cover with aluminum foil and let stand 5 minutes. Then slice loaf and spoon Creamy Mustard Sauce over slices. Garnish with chopped parsley and serve.

Serves 4.

Creamy Mustard Sauce While loaf is standing, in a 1-cup microwave-safe measure, combine sour cream and mustard. Microwave on high until warm (2 to 3 minutes).

Makes ¾ cup.

Serve a whole roasted chicken, golden from its sherry basting, with new potatoes and slender young carrots for an impressive family Sunday dinner.

... FOR MEATS

☐ Use a microwave-safe rack under roasts during cooking. If you don't have a rack, substitute a microwave-safe saucer or lid. In a pinch, several carrots or stalks of celery will work; just don't plan to serve them as vegetables.

☐ Roasts that are evenly shaped cook best in the microwave. If a roast has a thin end, cover it with aluminum foil partway through the cooking to prevent overcooking. Be sure foil does not touch sides of oven.

☐ Less tender cuts of meat should be cooked covered, either in a casserole or in a cooking bag. Add a small amount of liquid to create steam. (If you use a cooking bag, remember to tie it shut with a nonmetal closure, such as string or yarn. Make several slits in the bag to allow steam to escape.)

☐ Meats with some fat content, in the form of marbling, brown more evenly than very lean meat. Microwave browning agents are available to help those cuts that may not brown well.

☐ A microwave oven thermometer records the actual temperature of roasts. The same internal temperatures you use for conventional roasting apply to microwave-roasted meat. An instant-read thermometer can also be used: Remove the roast from the microwave and insert the thermometer for a reading in 10 seconds.

☐ Cover roasts with a tent of waxed paper to eliminate oven spattering. The waxed paper will also hold in some heat and steam to assist with the cooking. If you are concerned only with spattering, cover roasts with paper toweling to absorb grease.

FAMILY FAVORITE MEAT LOAF

Create a meat loaf ring by lightly packing the meat against the edge of a 9-inch-diameter microwave-safe baking dish or pie plate. Wad two squares of paper towels and place them in the center opening to absorb extra drippings while the meat loaf is cooking.

  1½ pounds ground beef
   1 egg, beaten
   2 slices fresh bread, broken into crumbs
   1 medium onion, chopped
   1 medium green bell pepper, chopped
   1 teaspoon salt
   ½ teaspoon freshly ground pepper

1. In a large bowl combine all ingredients. Mix lightly.

2. Form mixture into a ring as suggested above (or see Note). Microwave on high (100%) until meat is browned (10 to 12 minutes). Cover with aluminum foil and let stand 10 minutes.

Serves 4 or 5.

Note The meat loaf can also be shaped into a loaf and baked in a 5- by 9-inch microwave-safe loaf dish. Microwave on high until meat is browned (12 to 15 minutes). Cover with aluminum foil and let stand 5 minutes.

ALL-AMERICAN POT ROAST

Pot roasts are cuts of meat that require long cooking to tenderize. Using a low power level and a closed cooking bag produces a tasty, succulent roast. The cooking liquid may be thickened for gravy (see page 69).

   1 tablespoon flour
   ½ teaspoon paprika
   ½ teaspoon freshly ground pepper
   1 boneless chuck roast (2 to 3 lb)
   1 small onion, sliced
   ½ cup beef bouillon

1. In a small bowl combine flour, paprika, and pepper. Rub over all surfaces of roast.

2. Place roast in a cooking bag and set in a microwave-safe baking dish. Add onion and beef bouillon to bag. Tie bag closed with plastic strip or string, leaving steam hole about diameter of your finger.

3. Microwave on medium-low (30%) until roast is tender (32 to 38 minutes per pound), carefully turning bag over twice during cooking. Let roast stand in bag 15 minutes.

Serves 4 to 6.

SWEET AND SOUR BEEF

Serve this dish on a bed of hot buttered noodles. Complete the meal with corn on the cob (see page 45) and ice cream parfaits (see pages 97 and 100).

   1 tablespoon vegetable oil
  1½ to 2 pounds beef round, cut into 1-inch cubes
   ½ cup tomato sauce
   ¼ cup red wine vinegar
   1 teaspoon salt
   1 large onion, chopped
   ½ cup firmly packed brown sugar
   2 tablespoons Worcestershire sauce
   2 large carrots, cut into ¼-inch slices
      Hot buttered noodles, for accompaniment

1. In a 4-quart microwave-safe casserole, microwave oil on high (100%) until hot (2 to 3 minutes). Add beef, stirring to coat with oil, and microwave on high until beef is only slightly pink (6 to 7 minutes).

2. Add tomato sauce, vinegar, salt, onion, brown sugar, Worcestershire sauce, and carrots. Cover and microwave on high until mixture boils (5 to 6 minutes), stirring once.

3. Reduce power to medium (50%) and microwave until carrots and beef are tender (5 to 7 minutes). Let stand, covered, 10 minutes. Serve over hot buttered noodles.

Serves 4 to 6.

LEMON-MINT LAMB CHOPS

Serve these tender chops on a bed of fresh mint leaves from the garden.

> 1 tablespoon vegetable oil
> 8 loin lamb chops
> ¼ cup lemon juice
> 1 tablespoon chopped fresh mint, for sprinkling
> Lemon slices, for garnish

1. Preheat a microwave browning dish in the microwave on high (100%) until hot (6 minutes). Add oil and microwave on high until oil is hot (1 to 2 minutes). Swirl oil to coat dish and add 4 of the chops. Microwave on high until chops are browned on the bottom (2 to 3 minutes). Turn chops over and microwave on high until chops are browned and tender (1½ to 3 minutes). Remove to platter and set aside.

2. Again preheat browning dish in microwave on high until hot (2 to 3 minutes). Add remaining 4 lamb chops and microwave as in step 1.

3. Place all chops in browning dish and pour lemon juice over them. Microwave on high until juice is warm (1 to 2 minutes). Remove chops to serving platter, pour warm lemon juice over chops, sprinkle with mint, and garnish with lemon slices. Serve immediately.

Serves 4.

CURRIED LAMB

Curries are fun to serve with several people gathered around the table. Place the condiments in small bowls and pass them.

> 2 tablespoons butter or margarine
> 1½ pounds lamb, cut into ½-inch cubes
> 1 cup coarsely chopped onion
> 1 tart apple, peeled and chopped
> 1 cup beef stock
> 2 tablespoons flour
> 1½ teaspoons curry powder
> ½ cup hot water
> Cooked rice, for accompaniment
> Selection of condiments, for accompaniment (see Note)

MEAT ROASTING GUIDE

This chart provides a guide to the microwave roasting times for some frequently cooked meats. Check the microwave cookbook for your oven for other cuts you may want to prepare.

Meat	Power Level	Cooking Time Per Pound
Tender Beef Roasts		
Rib, top round, tenderloin		
Rare	Medium (50%)	7 to 10 minutes
Medium	Medium (50%)	8 to 11 minutes
Well-done	Medium (50%)	9 to 12 minutes
Less Tender Roasts		
Rump, chuck brisket (should be covered during cooking)	Medium-low (30%)	25 to 32 minutes
Pork		
Loin	Medium (50%)	12 to 15 minutes
Fresh ham	Medium (50%)	11 to 13 minutes
Smoked ham	Medium (50%)	9 to 11 minutes
Lamb		
Leg	Medium (50%)	9 to 12 minutes
Shoulder	Medium (50%)	11 to 14 minutes
Veal		
Roast	Medium (50%)	12 to 16 minutes

1. In a 2-quart microwave-safe casserole, microwave butter on high (100%) until melted (30 to 60 seconds). Add lamb and microwave on high until meat is no longer pink (5 to 7 minutes).

2. Add onion and apple. Cover and microwave on high until softened (3 to 4 minutes). Add stock; cover and microwave on high until lamb is tender and stock is boiling (3 to 5 minutes).

3. Combine flour and curry powder with hot water. Stir into lamb mixture, cover, and microwave on high until liquid is slightly thickened (1 to 2 minutes). Serve on hot rice accompanied by small bowls of condiments.

Serves 4 or 5.

Note Suggested condiments include peanuts, sliced green onion, chutney, flaked coconut, diced cucumber, and raisins.

CHILI CON CARNE

If you like spicy chili, add extra chili powder. Serve the chili alone in bowls or over rice.

> 1 pound ground round
> 1 small onion, chopped
> 2 cups tomato purée or 1 can (15½ oz) tomato purée
> 1 teaspoon chili powder, or to taste
> ½ teaspoon salt
> ¼ teaspoon freshly ground pepper
> 1 can (16 oz) red kidney beans
> Grated Cheddar cheese, for garnish

1. In a 3-quart microwave-safe casserole, combine meat and onion. Microwave on high (100%) until meat is browned and onions are soft (3½ to 4½ minutes), stirring twice.

2. Stir in tomato purée, chili powder, salt, pepper, and beans. Cover and microwave on high until chili is hot (5 to 6 minutes). Let stand, covered, 5 minutes. Garnish with cheese.

Serves 4.

THE MICROWAVE-BOOSTED BARBECUE

Use your microwave to cut down on grilling time and keep you out of the kitchen. A microwave oven and a barbecue pit are wonderful partners: When designing an outdoor cooking space, consider a microwave as a permanent appliance in that area. You will find so many uses for it, you'll be glad you planned ahead.

☐ Precook chicken, ribs, and other barbecue items in the microwave. Finish on the grill for barbecue flavor in a shorter time.

☐ To produce well-done steaks without burning, barbecue the steak and then microwave it to order.

☐ Cook vegetable accompaniments, such as ratatouille and baked beans, in the microwave. For barbecue-style fresh corn on the cob, remove all but one layer of husk. Pull back remaining husk and remove silk. Brush corn with melted butter and replace remaining husk. Microwave on high (100%) until corn is tender (3 to 4 minutes per ear).

☐ In the microwave steam vegetables to include on your tray of crudités. Brussels sprouts, green beans, and cauliflower benefit from a short time in the microwave before being chilled; add 1 tablespoon water per cup vegetables, cover tightly, and microwave on high (100%) until vegetables are just slightly tender (30 to 60 seconds per cup).

☐ Microwave a dessert to serve at the barbecue without heating up the kitchen. Bake your favorite brownie recipe and top the brownies with Sinful Hot Fudge (see page 100), or make the Chocolate Frosted Brownies on page 93.

☐ Prepare your own barbecue sauce in the microwave and brush it on chicken or ribs while they are being barbecued.

☐ Cook extra burgers or steaks on the barbecue, then freeze and reheat in the microwave for a great outdoor barbecue taste. Reheat one frozen burger or steak on a plate, covered, on medium (50%) until hot (2 to 3 minutes). Do not overcook. This method works best for those who like their meats cooked medium to well-done.

☐ For a large party, barbecue chicken, sausage, or burgers ahead and reheat them in the microwave. You'll serve everyone more quickly and the chef can enjoy the party too.

☐ Make fresh condiments in your microwave to serve at the barbecue. Your Spicy Picnic Mustard (see page 117) and Sweet Hot Dog Relish (see page 121) may make you famous.

☐ Hamburgers and cheeseburgers can be microwave grilled on a browning dish. Form 4-ounce patties of even thickness. Preheat browning dish (see page 13) on high (100%) 5 minutes. Place patty on hot dish and microwave on high 1½ minutes. Turn over patty and microwave second side on high until browned and medium-rare (1 to 1½ minutes). To cook additional patties at the same time, add about 15 seconds per patty on each side. Top each with one cheese slice for last 30 seconds of cooking time, if desired.

SAUSAGE-AND-MUSHROOM–STUFFED FLANK STEAK

For a head start on dinner, marinate the steak overnight, but wait until just before cooking the steak to prepare the stuffing.

> 1 *flank steak (1½ to 2 lb)*
> ¼ *cup dry red wine*
> 1 *tablespoon lemon juice*
> 1 *tablespoon olive oil*
> 1 *clove garlic, minced*
> ½ *teaspoon freshly ground pepper*

Sausage-and-Mushroom Stuffing

> ½ *pound pork sausage*
> 1 *cup sliced mushrooms*
> 1 *small onion, chopped*
> 1½ *cups soft bread crumbs*

1. Place steak in a sealable plastic bag. Combine wine, lemon juice, oil, garlic, and pepper. Pour mixture over steak in bag and seal bag. Place bag in a flat baking dish and marinate in refrigerator at least 2 hours, or overnight.

2. Remove steak from marinade and place on a flat surface. Score steak lightly with a knife. Spread Sausage-and-Mushroom Stuffing on scored steak and roll up from wide side. Pin with wooden skewers or tie with string so roll retains shape during cooking.

3. Place steak roll in an 8- by 12-inch microwave-safe baking dish. Cover with waxed paper and microwave on high (100%) 8 minutes. Reduce power to medium (50%) and microwave until meat is tender (16 to 18 minutes). Let stand, covered, 5 minutes.

Serves 4 or 5.

Sausage-and-Mushroom Stuffing When ready to cook steak, in a medium bowl combine sausage, mushrooms, onion, and bread crumbs; stir until well blended.

Makes about 2 cups.

BAKED HAM STACK

You will find a surprise in the middle of these two layers of ham. This dish is destined to become a family favorite served with Easy Potatoes au Gratin (see page 47) and fresh broccoli.

    2 center-cut slices smoked ham
      (about 2 lb total)
    1 tablespoon prepared mustard
    1 tablespoon creamy peanut
      butter
    ½ cup pineapple juice
      Fresh pineapple spears,
      for garnish

1. In an 8- by 12-inch microwave-safe baking dish, place one slice of the ham. In a small bowl stir together mustard and peanut butter until smooth; spread evenly on ham slice. Top with second ham slice.

2. Cover with waxed paper and microwave on high (100%) until ham is warm (5 to 7 minutes).

3. Pour pineapple juice over ham. Cover with waxed paper and microwave on high until ham is hot (5 to 7 minutes), basting several times with juice from bottom of baking dish. Let stand, covered, 5 minutes. To serve, garnish with pineapple spears.

Serves 4 or 5.

VEAL PARMESAN

It is important to have the oil very hot when browning the cutlets to keep the cracker coating crispy.

    1 egg
    1 tablespoon milk
    1 cup dry cracker crumbs
    ½ teaspoon dried oregano
    1 to 1¼ pounds veal cutlets
      (6 to 8 cutlets), thinly sliced
    2 tablespoons vegetable oil
    6 to 8 slices mozzarella cheese
    2 cups spaghetti sauce
      Parmesan cheese, for
      sprinkling

1. In a pie plate beat together egg and milk. In a small bowl stir together cracker crumbs and oregano; turn onto waxed paper. Dip each

cutlet into egg mixture and then coat well with crumb mixture.

2. Preheat microwave browning dish in the microwave on high (100%) until hot (6 minutes). Add oil and microwave on high until oil is hot (1 to 2 minutes). Add cutlets and microwave on high until cutlets are browned on bottom (1½ to 2 minutes). Turn cutlets over and microwave on high to brown second side (1 to 1½ minutes).

3. Top each cutlet with 1 slice of cheese. Pour spaghetti sauce over cutlets. Cover with waxed paper, making sure paper does not touch hot surface of tray, and microwave on high until sauce is hot (3 to 4 minutes). Let cutlets stand, covered, on heatproof surface 5 minutes. Sprinkle with Parmesan and serve.

Serves 4.

Marinate the flank steak, then roll it with a Sausage-and-Mushroom Stuffing for a delicious entrée prepared in less time than you would think. Serve it with tasty Mexican Salsa (see page 120) and South-of-the-Border Corn Bread (see page 33).

WINTER EVENING REPAST

Herbed Roast Pork

Orange-Baked Sweet Potatoes

Sautéed Zucchini Rounds

Coleslaw

Scalloped Pineapple

Fresh Apple Cider

Good food, good friends, and a roaring fire add up to a perfect evening. Here is a menu that serves four to six to fit the occasion. The herbs rubbed on the roast give it a robust flavor; bake the potatoes while the roast is standing. For the perfect accompaniments, prepare your favorite coleslaw and sauté young, small zucchini. Peel the zucchini, if desired, slice, and place in a microwave-safe dish with butter. Cover zucchini and microwave on high (100%) until crisp-tender; season to taste.

HERBED ROAST PORK

Roast pork is temptingly succulent when it is roasted in the microwave. If you prefer a crispy brown surface, place the roast under the conventional broiler during the 10-minute standing time.

>   1 small onion, finely minced
> ½ teaspoon ground sage
> ¼ teaspoon ground thyme
> ¼ teaspoon freshly ground pepper
>   1 boneless pork loin (about 3 lb)

1. In a small bowl combine onion, sage, thyme, and pepper. Rub over entire surface of pork, allowing pieces of onion to cling to surface of meat.

2. Place a microwave rack in a 9-inch-square microwave-safe baking dish. Place meat on rack, cover with waxed paper, and microwave on medium (50%) until microwave meat thermometer registers 160° F (12 to 14 minutes per pound).

3. Cover roast with aluminum foil and let stand 10 minutes. Slice roast and serve.

Serves 4 to 6.

ORANGE-BAKED SWEET POTATOES

The orange sauce continues to thicken while the sweet potato slices are cooking. Spoon the sauce over the sweet potatoes during cooking for an attractive orange glaze.

>   4 medium sweet potatoes
>   3 tablespoons butter
> ¼ cup firmly packed brown sugar
>   1 cup orange juice
>   2 teaspoons cornstarch
>   2 tablespoons bourbon

1. Wash sweet potatoes and prick with a fork. Place potatoes in circle on a paper towel–covered microwave-safe plate. Microwave on high (100%) until potatoes yield slightly when squeezed (10 to 12 minutes). Let cool.

2. Meanwhile, in a 2-cup microwave-safe measure, combine butter and brown sugar. Microwave on high until butter melts (30 to 60 seconds). Stir to mix.

3. In a small bowl combine orange juice and cornstarch. Stir into butter mixture, blending well. Microwave on high until sauce is thickened (1½ to 3 minutes). Stir in bourbon.

4. Peel cooled sweet potatoes and cut into ¼-inch-thick slices. Place slices in a 2-quart microwave-safe casserole. Pour orange sauce over top. Microwave on high until potatoes are soft and sauce is hot (3 to 5 minutes). Let stand 5 minutes.

Serves 4 to 6.

SCALLOPED PINEAPPLE

This is a dish with a dual role. It is delicious served warm as a side dish with ham or pork or served chilled with whipped cream for dessert.

> ¼ cup butter or margarine
> ¾ cup sugar
>   1 egg
>   2 cups cubed white bread (about 3 slices)
>   1 can (8 oz) crushed pineapple, undrained
>   Whipped cream, for accompaniment (optional)

1. In a medium bowl cream butter and sugar. Beat in egg. Fold in bread cubes and pineapple.

2. Spread mixture in an 8-inch-diameter microwave-safe baking dish. Microwave on high (100%) until bread is softened and pineapple is hot (4 to 5 minutes). Let stand 5 minutes before serving. To serve cold, chill in refrigerator at least 2 hours; serve with whipped cream, if desired.

Serves 4 to 6.

Pork roast and sweet potatoes give a cozy feeling to a winter dinner with friends. Serve warm apple cider and Scalloped Pineapple for dessert.

This mint-filled chocolate cake roll (see page 87) is a stunning dessert when served in a pool of vanilla and strawberry sauce (both recipes on page 100).

Delectable Desserts

The popularity of dessert never seems to diminish. From delectable Hummingbird Cake (see page 84) and fluffy Orange Chiffon Pie (see page 95) to down-home favorites such as Chocolate Frosted Brownies (see page 93) and warm Old-fashioned Gingerbread (see page 89), delicious desserts are awaited impatiently by guests and family alike. A microwave oven makes the desserts in this chapter so simple that excuses for omitting this winning course will be hard to find.

CAKES

Cakes baked in the microwave are moist and tender. As with any cake, however, be sure to wrap microwaved cake leftovers well to prevent them from drying out.

CARROT CAKE WITH CREAM CHEESE FROSTING

This dessert is sized for small families, but if there are any leftovers, store them tightly wrapped in the refrigerator.

1 cup grated carrots
1 cup flour
1 cup sugar
¾ teaspoon baking soda
½ teaspoon baking powder
¼ teaspoon salt
1 teaspoon ground cinnamon
1 teaspoon ground ginger
2 eggs, beaten
¼ cup vegetable oil
½ teaspoon vanilla extract

Cream Cheese Frosting

1 package (3 oz) cream cheese
1 tablespoon butter or margarine
¼ teaspoon vanilla extract
1 cup sifted confectioners' sugar

1. In a large mixing bowl, combine carrots, flour, sugar, baking soda, baking powder, salt, cinnamon, and ginger. Beat in egg, oil, and vanilla.

2. Lightly grease a 9-inch-diameter microwave-safe baking dish. Pour batter into prepared dish, smoothing top. Microwave on medium-high (70%) until sides loosen from dish and a toothpick inserted in center comes out clean (7 to 10 minutes). Let cool, then frost with Cream Cheese Frosting.

Serves 6 to 8.

Cream Cheese Frosting In a medium microwave-safe mixing bowl, combine cream cheese and butter. Microwave on high (100%) until softened (30 to 60 seconds). Stir in vanilla. Add confectioners' sugar and mix well.

Makes about 1 cup.

GRAND MARNIER CREAM TORTE

Prepare this torte early in the day so it will be well chilled when you are ready to serve it. Cut the torte into small wedges—this dessert is rich.

¼ cup butter or margarine, softened (see page 87)
⅓ cup sugar
1½ teaspoons vanilla extract
3 squares (1 oz each) semisweet chocolate, melted and cooled (see page 87)
3 eggs
⅓ cup flour
2 tablespoons chopped pecans
3 tablespoons Grand Marnier liqueur
1½ cups whipped cream

1. Lightly grease a 9-inch-square microwave-safe baking dish; set aside. In a large mixing bowl, cream softened butter, sugar, and vanilla until fluffy. Beat in chocolate and eggs. Stir in flour.

2. Pour batter into prepared dish, smoothing top. Sprinkle with pecans. Microwave on medium (50%) until a toothpick inserted in center comes out clean (8 to 10 minutes). Let cool completely.

3. Slice cooled cake horizontally into 2 layers. Brush cut sides with 2 tablespoons of the Grand Marnier. Fold the remaining 1 tablespoon liqueur into whipped cream. Reserve ½ cup of the whipped cream for garnish and spread remaining whipped cream on first layer. Cover with second layer. Pipe reserved whipped cream decoratively around edges of torte (see Note). Refrigerate until ready to serve.

Serves 8 to 10.

Note To pipe whipped cream around edges of torte, use a pastry bag fitted with a star tip.

HUMMINGBIRD CAKE

This rich pineapple and banana cake is a southern tradition.

1 cup finely ground pecans
2¼ cups flour
1¼ cups sugar
½ teaspoon salt
1 teaspoon baking soda
1 teaspoon ground cinnamon
3 eggs, beaten
½ cup vegetable oil
1 teaspoon vanilla extract
1 can (8 oz) crushed pineapple, undrained
2 medium-sized ripe bananas, peeled and chopped

Confectioners' Sugar Glaze

1 cup sifted confectioners' sugar
2 to 4 tablespoons milk

1. Grease a 12-cup microwave-safe bundt cake dish and sprinkle with ¼ cup of the pecans. Set aside.

2. In a large mixing bowl, combine flour, sugar, salt, baking soda, and cinnamon. Add eggs and vegetable oil and blend until dry ingredients are moistened. Stir in vanilla, pineapple with its juice, bananas, and remaining ¾ cup pecans.

3. Pour batter into prepared dish. Microwave on medium (50%) 9 minutes, rotating dish twice. Then microwave on high (100%) until cake loosens from sides of pan and top appears dry (4 to 6 minutes). Let stand directly on heatproof surface 10 minutes. Invert cake onto serving plate. Drizzle with Confectioners' Sugar Glaze, allowing glaze to drip decoratively down sides of cake.

Serves 10 to 12.

Confectioners' Sugar Glaze In a small bowl combine confectioners' sugar and milk, stirring until thoroughly combined and glaze is smooth.

Makes about ¾ cup.

Moist, rich, fruity, and drizzled with a smooth confectioners' sugar glaze, Hummingbird Cake is a stunning finale to an elegant dinner party.

Chocolate Pudding Cake— more like pudding than cake—is a deliciously rich dessert. Serve it in individual dishes and crown it with dollops of sweetened whipped cream.

CHOCOLATE PUDDING CAKE

This fudgy cake forms a pudding base as it bakes. Scoop it into dessert dishes rather than trying to cut it into cake slices. Top with sweetened whipped cream if you like, but it is rich enough to be served alone.

- 1 cup flour
- ¼ cup sugar
- 2 tablespoons plus ¼ cup cocoa
- 2 teaspoons baking powder
- ½ teaspoon salt
- ½ cup milk
- 2 tablespoons vegetable oil
- 1 teaspoon vanilla extract
- ½ cup chopped pecans (optional)
- ¾ cup firmly packed brown sugar
- 1¼ cups hot water

1. Lightly grease an 8-inch-diameter microwave-safe baking dish; set aside. In a large bowl combine flour, sugar, the 2 tablespoons cocoa, baking powder, and salt. Add milk, oil, and vanilla, mixing well. Pour batter into prepared dish. Sprinkle with pecans, if used.

2. In a small bowl combine brown sugar, the ¼ cup cocoa, and the water. Pour mixture slowly over top of batter. Microwave on high (100%) until bubbles on surface of cake have broken (6 to 7½ minutes). Let stand 5 minutes. Spoon into dessert dishes and serve warm.

Serves 6.

PEPPERMINT CAKE ROLL

The mint filling in this cake roll is a pleasant surprise. Allow at least an hour for the cake to chill before serving it.

- 4 eggs
- ¾ cup sugar
- ¾ cup flour
- ¼ cup cocoa
- ¾ teaspoon baking powder
- 1 teaspoon vanilla extract
- 2 tablespoons confectioners' sugar, for sprinkling towel
- 1 box (5½ oz) chocolate-covered mint patties
- 1 cup sweetened whipped cream

1. Line an 8- by 12-inch microwave-safe baking dish with waxed paper cut to fit; set aside. In a large bowl beat eggs until thick and lemon colored. Add sugar, flour, cocoa, baking powder, and vanilla. Beat until well blended.

2. Pour batter into prepared dish and spread evenly. Microwave on high (100%) 2 minutes. Shield corners of dish with 2-inch-wide strips of aluminum foil and microwave again on high until bubbles on surface have broken and surface appears dry (3 to 4 minutes).

3. Lay a clean dish towel on a flat working surface; sprinkle towel with confectioners' sugar. Immediately turn cake out onto sugared towel and remove waxed paper from cake. Roll up cake starting at long edge. Let cool while rolled.

4. Meanwhile, in a small microwave-safe mixing bowl, microwave mint patties on medium (50%) until soft (1 to 3 minutes). Stir until smooth.

5. Unroll cake and spread with warm mint filling. Spread whipped cream over mint filling. Roll up filled cake and chill at least 1 hour or until ready to serve.

Serves 6 to 8.

... FOR MICROWAVE BAKING

The microwave oven can be your chief assistant whether you are baking conventionally or in the microwave. Melting butter and chocolate, toasting nuts, heating a jelly glaze, and baking a cookie crumb crust are all accomplished easily and quickly in a microwave oven. Here are some tips to get you started.

☐ Remember to use your microwave to prepare butter or margarine when baking. Use the medium-power setting (50%) to soften and high power (100%) to melt. The time depends on how much butter is heated. Less than ½ cup usually requires less than 1 minute; for larger amounts, add time in 30-second increments. Watch carefully; the difference between softened and melted butter may be only a few seconds.

☐ Enhance the flavor of nuts by toasting them in the microwave. Spread shelled nuts in a shallow baking dish and microwave on high (100%) 2 to 3 minutes per cup, stirring twice. Watch carefully; the oil in nuts heats rapidly and can produce a burned taste. Your nose should be your guide as you smell the nuts toasting.

☐ Microwaved baked products usually do not brown during the short time required for baking. Nuts, spices, cookie crumbs, and frosting or glazes assist in producing an eye-appealing finished product.

☐ In microwave recipes that call for greasing a shallow baking dish, you may prefer to line the dish with waxed paper to make greasing unnecessary.

☐ If a conventional recipe requires greasing and flouring the dish, grease but do not flour when converting to microwave cooking. Microwave baked products cook so quickly that the flour is not absorbed into the batter and remains as an unattractive coating on the surface. If you want to use a coating, try cinnamon and sugar, ground nuts, or finely crushed cookies.

☐ Chocolate is easily melted in the microwave, but be aware that it doesn't change shape until you stir it! Microwave chocolate on high (100%) and stir every 30 to 60 seconds until it is completely melted. The surface will become shiny as it heats. Overcooking will harden chocolate and make it difficult to blend well.

☐ You can prepare your favorite cookie crumb crust in the microwave. Press the crumbs into a microwave-safe pie plate and microwave on high (100%) until set (2 to 4 minutes). Let cool and fill with your favorite filling. This cooked dessert can be made without heating up the kitchen on a hot day.

☐ Heat jelly in the microwave to glaze a fruit tart. The high sugar content of the jelly allows it to heat in 1 to 2 minutes on high power (100%).

☐ Cakes will rise uniformly if you rotate the dish once or twice during baking. Do this even if your oven has a turntable.

Tips

... FOR SERVING MICROWAVE DESSERTS

☐ Reheating pies, cakes, and cobblers in the microwave is the perfect way to serve them warm (see reheating chart on page 12). Cover baked goods lightly with a paper towel, paper napkin, or waxed paper to protect them from drying. Microwave on high (100%) for 10 to 20 seconds per serving, or until they just feel warm to the touch. If you heat them so they feel hot, they will become hard during the few minutes it takes you to serve them.

☐ Here is a fun tip for pie à la mode. Place a scoop of cold ice cream on a slice of room-temperature pie. Microwave on high (100%) 15 seconds. The pie will be warm and the ice cream will still be perched on top. Be sure to let your guests watch this phenomenon!

☐ Connoisseurs of soft ice cream microwave the container of ice cream 15 to 30 seconds on medium (50%) to make it easier to scoop and smoother to eat.

☐ Store dessert sauces in microwave-safe containers in the refrigerator. Heat the sauce in the microwave on high (100%) until hot (1 to 3 minutes). Pour sauce over ice cream or cake and return leftover sauce to the refrigerator in the same container.

☐ Sugar heats quickly in the microwave, so the sweet fillings in microwave cakes, rolls, or doughnuts will be much hotter than the bread around them. Use caution when biting into these products after microwave reheating.

☐ Prepared pudding mixes are easy to cook in the microwave. Use a 4-cup microwave-safe measure. Combine pudding mix and milk, following package directions. Microwave on high (100%) until pudding is thickened (4 to 5 minutes), stirring twice. Cooking does not require constant stirring and there are no lumps.

☐ To prepare a fast frosting for cakes and cookies, use grated chocolate candy bars or chocolate chips. Sprinkle on the surface of the baked product and microwave on high (100%) until chocolate is shiny (1 to 2 minutes). Spread melted chocolate over surface with a spatula.

PINEAPPLE-SPICE UPSIDE-DOWN CAKE

Center a stemmed cherry in each pineapple ring, as in the photograph at left, to make this down-home dessert a dramatic presentation.

> 1 can (16 oz) pineapple rings, undrained
> 6 tablespoons butter or margarine, plus ⅓ cup butter or margarine, softened (see page 87)
> 1 cup firmly packed brown sugar
> ½ cup granulated sugar
> 1 egg
> 1½ cups flour
> 1 teaspoon baking soda
> 1 teaspoon ground cinnamon
> ¾ teaspoon ground ginger
> ¼ teaspoon salt

1. Drain pineapple rings, reserving ⅓ cup of the juice.

2. In a 9-inch-diameter microwave-safe baking dish, microwave the 6 tablespoons butter on high (100%) until melted (1 to 2 minutes). Add ¾ cup of the brown sugar and stir until smooth. Spread mixture evenly in bottom of dish. Arrange drained pineapple rings in decorative design. Set aside.

3. In a large mixing bowl, beat the ⅓ cup butter, granulated sugar, and the remaining ¼ cup brown sugar until light and fluffy. Beat in egg.

4. In a small bowl combine flour, baking soda, cinnamon, ginger, and salt. Stir into butter mixture alternately with reserved pineapple juice until well blended. Spoon batter over pineapple rings, spreading evenly.

5. Microwave on high until top of cake appears dry and cake loosens from sides of dish (6 to 8 minutes). Let stand directly on heatproof surface 10 minutes. Invert cake onto serving plate. Serve chilled or warm.

Serves 6 to 8.

OLD-FASHIONED GINGERBREAD

Assemble the batter and put the gingerbread in the microwave just as you sit down for dinner. It will bake, stand the required time, and be ready to serve when dinner is finished. Or to reheat entire cake, see Note.

    2   eggs, beaten
    ⅓   cup sugar
    ½   cup vegetable oil
    ⅓   cup dark molasses
    1   teaspoon baking powder
    ½   teaspoon baking soda
    ½   teaspoon salt
    1½ teaspoons ground ginger
    ½   teaspoon ground cloves
    ½   teaspoon ground cinnamon
    1½ cups flour
    ½   cup sour cream
        Sweetened whipped cream
        (optional)

1. Lightly grease a 9-inch-square microwave-safe baking dish; set aside. In a large mixing bowl, combine eggs, sugar, vegetable oil, and molasses until well blended. Stir in baking powder, baking soda, salt, ginger, cloves, and cinnamon, mixing thoroughly. Add flour alternately with sour cream. Stir until just well blended.

2. Pour batter into prepared dish and smooth top. Microwave on high (100%) until top appears dry and cake loosens from sides of dish (7 to 9 minutes). Let stand directly on heatproof surface 10 minutes. Cut into 3-inch squares and serve warm with whipped cream, if desired.

Serves 9.

<u>Note</u> Reheat whole cake on high until cake feels just warm to the touch (30 to 40 seconds).

Memories of grandmother's kitchen are evoked by the tantalizing aroma of Old-fashioned Gingerbread, drizzled with Rich Vanilla Sauce (see page 100) and topped with whipped cream.

ZUCCHINI CRUMB CAKE

Zucchini gives this cake a moist texture. To make the cake out of season, grate zucchini and freeze it during the summer, when it is abundant in the market and in home gardens.

> 1 cup sugar
> ⅔ cup vegetable oil
> ½ teaspoon vanilla extract
> 2 eggs
> 1¼ cups flour
> ½ teaspoon salt
> 1¼ teaspoons baking soda
> 1½ teaspoons ground cinnamon
> 1 cup grated peeled zucchini

Crumb Topping

> ¼ cup sugar
> ¼ cup chopped walnuts
> 3 ounces semisweet chocolate chips

1. In a medium mixing bowl, combine sugar, oil, vanilla, and eggs until well mixed. Add flour, salt, baking soda, and cinnamon, stirring until blended. Fold in zucchini.

2. Pour batter into a lightly greased 9-inch-diameter microwave-safe baking dish. Microwave on medium (50%) 6 minutes, rotating dish once. Microwave on high (100%) until top appears dry (2 to 3 minutes). Sprinkle Crumb Topping evenly over cake. Microwave on high until chocolate appears shiny (1 to 2 minutes). Let stand directly on heatproof surface until cool.

Serves 6 to 8.

Crumb Topping In a small bowl combine sugar, walnuts, and chocolate chips until well mixed.

Makes about ¾ cup.

COOKIES

Bar cookies can be baked in minutes as a delicious addition to a packed school lunch. They're easy enough for children to prepare for a special after-school snack.

TART LEMON BARS

These thin, layered bars are an elegant conclusion to a special dinner. Their tart yet sweet taste is welcomingly refreshing after a hearty meal or on a hot summer night.

> 1 cup sugar
> 1 tablespoon grated lemon rind
> 2 eggs
> 1 tablespoon flour
> ½ teaspoon baking powder
> ¼ teaspoon salt
> ⅓ cup lemon juice
> Confectioners' sugar, for dusting

Lemon Crust

> ¼ cup sugar
> 2 tablespoons grated lemon rind
> 1 cup flour
> ⅓ cup butter or margarine

1. Prepare Lemon Crust. Then, in a medium mixing bowl, combine sugar and lemon rind. Beat in eggs, flour, baking powder, and salt. Stir in lemon juice until batter is well mixed.

2. Pour batter over Lemon Crust. Microwave on medium (50%) until surface is firm (8 to 10 minutes). Let cool, then cut into bars. Dust tops with confectioners' sugar.

Makes 16 bars.

Lemon Crust In a medium mixing bowl, combine sugar, lemon rind, and flour. Cut in butter until mixture is crumbly. Press into an ungreased 9-inch-square microwave-safe baking dish. Microwave crust on high (100%) until surface appears dry (3 to 4 minutes).

A light dusting of confectioners' sugar enhances perfectly the slightly tart flavor of these classic lemon bars. Serve them with iced tea for a refreshing treat.

A favorite of young and old, Chocolate Frosted Brownies are a perfect snack when served with an ice-cold glass of milk.

CHOCOLATE PEANUT BARS

This bar cookie is a snap to prepare. Use butterscotch or chocolate mint chips as a variation.

- ½ cup butter or margarine
- ½ cup firmly packed brown sugar
- ½ cup flour
- ¾ cup flaked coconut
- ¼ teaspoon baking soda
- ½ cup semisweet chocolate chips
- ¼ cup light corn syrup
- 1 tablespoon creamy peanut butter
- 1¼ cups salted peanuts

1. In a medium microwave-safe mixing bowl, microwave butter on high (100%) until melted (30 to 60 seconds). Stir in brown sugar until smooth. Add flour, coconut, and baking soda and mix well.

2. Spread mixture evenly in an ungreased 9-inch-square microwave-safe baking dish. Microwave on high until surface appears bubbly (3 to 5 minutes). Let stand 5 minutes.

3. In a 4-cup microwave-safe measure, combine chocolate chips, corn syrup, and peanut butter. Microwave on high until chocolate is melted (1 to 2 minutes), stirring twice. Stir in peanuts. Spread chocolate mixture evenly over coconut base. Let cool completely. Cut into bars.

Makes 16 bars.

GLAZED APPLE-ORANGE BARS

These tasty, cakelike bars pack easily in lunch bags and stay fresh for several days tightly covered.

- 1 cup flour
- ½ teaspoon ground cinnamon
- ¼ teaspoon each *baking soda, salt, and ground nutmeg*
- 2 tablespoons butter or margarine, *softened (see page 87)*
- ⅓ cup granulated sugar
- 2 tablespoons molasses
- 1 egg
- ½ cup applesauce
- 1 teaspoon grated orange rind

Orange Juice Glaze

- 1 cup sifted confectioners' sugar
- 1 tablespoon orange juice

1. In a small bowl combine flour, cinnamon, baking soda, salt, and nutmeg. Set aside.

2. In a medium bowl cream butter and granulated sugar until light and fluffy. Beat in molasses and egg. Stir in flour mixture, applesauce, and orange rind until well combined.

3. Pour batter into an ungreased 9-inch-square microwave-safe baking dish. Microwave on high (100%) until top appears dry and toothpick inserted in center comes out clean (5 to 7 minutes). Let cool in dish. Cut into bars and drizzle with Orange Juice Glaze.

Makes 16 bars.

Orange Juice Glaze In a small bowl combine confectioners' sugar and orange juice until smooth.

Makes about 1 cup.

CINNAMON CONFETTI BARS

Kids love these treats in school lunches. Look for spiced gumdrops to use for an even snappier flavor.

- ¾ cup butter or margarine
- ¾ cup sugar
- 1 egg
- ½ teaspoon vanilla extract
- 2¼ cups flour
- ½ teaspoon baking powder
- 1 teaspoon ground cinnamon
- ¼ teaspoon salt
- 1 package (8 oz) gumdrops (about 1 cup), chopped

1. In a large microwave-safe mixing bowl, microwave butter on medium (50%) until soft (30 to 60 seconds). Beat in sugar, egg, and vanilla.

2. In a medium bowl combine flour, baking powder, cinnamon, and salt. Stir flour mixture into butter mixture until well blended. Fold in gumdrops.

3. Spread batter in an ungreased 9-inch-square microwave-safe baking dish. Microwave on high (100%) until surface appears dry and evenly puffed (6 to 7 minutes).

4. Let stand directly on heatproof surface. When cool, cut into bars. Store tightly covered.

Makes 16 bars.

CHOCOLATE FROSTED BROWNIES

Chocolate frosting makes these fudgy brownies extra rich.

- ½ cup butter or margarine
- 1½ cups flour
- 1 cup sugar
- ¼ cup cocoa
- ¼ teaspoon salt
- 2 eggs, beaten
- 1 teaspoon vanilla extract

Chocolate Buttercream Frosting

- 2 tablespoons butter or margarine
- 2 tablespoons cocoa
- 1½ cups sifted confectioners' sugar

1. Lightly grease a 9-inch-square microwave-safe baking dish; set aside. In a small microwave-safe bowl, microwave butter on high (100%) until melted (1 to 2 minutes); reserve.

2. In a large bowl combine flour, sugar, cocoa, and salt. Add eggs, vanilla, and reserved melted butter, stirring until well mixed.

3. Spread batter in prepared dish. Microwave on high until top appears dry (6 to 8 minutes). Let cool directly on heatproof surface. Spread Chocolate Buttercream Frosting on cooled brownies. Cut into squares.

Makes 16 squares.

Chocolate Buttercream Frosting In a large microwave-safe bowl, microwave butter on high until melted (30 to 60 seconds). Add cocoa and confectioners' sugar; beat until thoroughly mixed and fluffy.

Makes about 1 cup.

GLAZED PEANUT BUTTER BARS

If you are looking for a cookie to mail, these firm, slightly crunchy bars are excellent. Just wrap each one individually in plastic to prevent drying out.

- ½ cup butter or margarine, softened (see page 87)
- ½ cup granulated sugar
- ½ cup firmly packed brown sugar
- 1 egg
- ⅓ cup creamy peanut butter
- ½ teaspoon baking soda
- ¼ teaspoon salt
- ½ teaspoon vanilla extract
- 1 cup flour
- 1 cup quick-cooking oatmeal
- 1 package (6 oz) semisweet chocolate chips

Peanut Butter Glaze

- ½ cup sifted confectioners' sugar
- ½ cup crunchy peanut butter
- 2 to 4 tablespoons milk

1. In a large bowl cream butter, granulated sugar, and brown sugar until fluffy. Beat in egg, creamy peanut butter, baking soda, salt, and vanilla. Add flour and oatmeal, mixing well.

2. Spread batter in a lightly greased 9-inch-square microwave-safe baking dish. Microwave on high (100%) until top appears dry and toothpick inserted in center comes out clean (6 to 8 minutes).

3. Sprinkle with chocolate chips. Microwave on high just until chocolate is shiny and soft (1 to 2 minutes). With a spatula spread softened chocolate over surface. Drizzle Peanut Butter Glaze over chocolate. Let cool completely, then cut into bars.

Makes 16 bars.

Peanut Butter Glaze In a small bowl combine confectioners' sugar, crunchy peanut butter, and enough milk to make a thin glaze. Stir until well mixed.

Makes about 1 cup.

PIES AND PUDDINGS

A microwave oven eliminates having to stir puddings constantly and produces lump-free results.

OZARK APPLE PUDDING

Top this warm pudding with a scoop of Rich Vanilla Ice Cream (see page 97) to enhance the apple flavor.

- 1 egg
- ½ cup sugar
- ½ teaspoon vanilla extract
- ⅓ cup flour
- 1 teaspoon baking powder
- 2 medium cooking apples, peeled, cored, and finely chopped (about 2 cups)
- ½ cup coarsely chopped walnuts
  Rich Vanilla Ice Cream (see page 97), optional

1. Lightly grease an 8-inch-diameter microwave-safe baking dish; set aside. In a medium mixing bowl, combine egg, sugar, and vanilla, beating until fluffy. Combine flour and baking powder; fold into butter mixture. Fold in apples and walnuts.

2. Spread apple mixture in prepared dish. Microwave on high (100%) until apples are tender (6 to 8 minutes). Let stand 10 minutes. Serve warm, topped with a scoop of Rich Vanilla Ice Cream, if desired.

Serves 4 to 6.

SMOOTH EGG CUSTARD

For a decorative touch bake this custard in small individual microwave-safe soufflé dishes.

- 2 cups milk
- 1 teaspoon vanilla extract
- 3 eggs
- ⅓ cup sugar
  Freshly ground nutmeg, for sprinkling

1. In a 4-cup microwave-safe measure, combine milk and vanilla. Microwave on high (100%) until very hot but not boiling (3 to 5 minutes).

2. In a large bowl beat eggs; gradually beat in sugar. Slowly pour hot milk mixture into egg mixture, beating continuously until well combined.

3. Divide mixture among four 1-cup soufflé dishes or 1-cup custard cups. Sprinkle with nutmeg. Arrange cups in circular pattern in the microwave. Microwave on low (10%) until custard is nearly set and knife inserted in center comes out clean (20 to 25 minutes). Let sit at least 1 hour; custard will firm as it sits.

Serves 4.

DUTCH APPLE PIE

Pick the fruit for this pie on a fall outing to the apple orchard.

- 6 cups cooking apples, peeled, cored, and sliced
- 1 cup sugar
- 2 tablespoons cornstarch
- ½ teaspoon ground cinnamon
- ¼ teaspoon ground nutmeg
- 1 tablespoon butter or margarine
- 1 baked pie shell (9 in.), in glass pie plate
  Cheddar cheese wedges, for garnish

Crumbly Topping

- ¾ cup firmly packed brown sugar
- ½ cup flour
- 1 teaspoon ground cinnamon
- ¼ cup butter or margarine

1. In a 3-quart microwave-safe casserole, combine apples, sugar, cornstarch, cinnamon, and nutmeg. Cover and microwave on high (100%) until apples are tender (6 to 8 minutes), stirring twice. Stir in butter. Pour into baked pie shell. Cover with Crumbly Topping, spreading topping evenly to edges of pie shell.

2. When ready to serve, microwave pie on high until it is warm (2 to 3 minutes). Cut into slices and garnish each with a cheese wedge.

Serves 6 to 8.

Crumbly Topping In a medium mixing bowl, combine brown sugar, flour, and cinnamon. Cut in butter until crumbly.

Makes about 1½ cups.

ORANGE CHIFFON PIE

This pie is also delicious with a graham cracker or vanilla cookie crumb crust.

    1 cup sugar
    ¼ cup cornstarch
    1¾ cups water
    1 egg, beaten
    ½ cup orange juice
    1½ cups whipped cream
    1 baked pie shell (9 in.)
    1 tablespoon slivered orange
       zest, for garnish

1. In a 2-quart microwave-safe dish, combine sugar, cornstarch, and the water, stirring until mixed. Microwave on high (100%) until boiling (5 to 7 minutes).

2. Slowly pour in beaten egg, stirring rapidly. Microwave on high until pudding boils (1 to 2 minutes), stirring once. Let cool.

3. Stir orange juice into cooled pudding. Fold in whipped cream. Mound filling in pie shell. Sprinkle with slivered orange zest and refrigerate at least 1 hour before serving.

Serves 6 to 8.

Cook the pudding for elegant Orange Chiffon Pie in the microwave, then pour it into a baked pie shell and chill. Garnish with slivers of orange zest and serve for a cool treat on a warm evening.

MICROWAVE ICE CREAM

Ice cream in the microwave? Strange as it seems, many ice creams are made from a cooked base that is chilled thoroughly in the refrigerator before being moved to the ice cream freezer. An ice cream base cooked in the microwave does not require constant stirring. Prepare the cooked base a day ahead and chill it thoroughly for maximum volume when freezing. The completed mixtures keep up to 3 days in the refrigerator. The ice cream keeps up to one week in the freezer.

CHOCOLATE DREAMS ICE CREAM

This rich chocolate ice cream is perfect for ice cream cones.

    2 eggs
    1 cup sugar
    1½ cups milk
    3 squares (1 oz each)
        semisweet chocolate, melted
        (see page 87)
    2 cups whipping cream
    1 teaspoon vanilla extract

1. In a large microwave-safe bowl, beat eggs and sugar until mixture is thick and lemon colored. Add milk and beat well. Microwave on medium (50%) until mixture is thickened (7 to 9 minutes), stirring twice. Stir in melted chocolate until thoroughly mixed. Chill in refrigerator about 30 minutes.

2. Stir in cream and vanilla. Chill in refrigerator 2 to 3 hours. Freeze according to ice cream freezer manufacturer's directions.

Makes 1 quart.

RICH VANILLA ICE CREAM

Serve this all-American treat with Sinful Hot Fudge (see page 100) or over Flaming Cherries Jubilee (see page 104).

    3 eggs
    ¾ cup sugar
    2 cups milk
    2 cups whipping cream
    1 tablespoon vanilla extract

1. In a large microwave-safe bowl, beat eggs and sugar until mixture is thick and lemon colored. Add milk and beat well. Microwave mixture on medium (50%) until slightly thickened (7 to 9 minutes). Chill mixture in refrigerator about 30 minutes.

2. Stir in cream and vanilla. Chill in refrigerator 2 to 3 hours. Freeze according to ice cream freezer manufacturer's directions.

Makes 1 quart.

FRESH STRAWBERRY ICE CREAM

Crushing the strawberries gives this ice cream a lovely pink color.

    1 cup granulated sugar
    ½ cup water
    1 pint ripe strawberries,
        washed and hulled
    1 tablespoon confectioners'
        sugar
    2 cups light cream
    1 teaspoon vanilla extract

1. In a 4-cup microwave-safe measure, combine granulated sugar and the water. Microwave on high (100%) until mixture boils and sugar is completely dissolved (4 to 6 minutes). Chill in refrigerator about 30 minutes.

2. In a medium bowl lightly crush strawberries with a fork. Stir in confectioners' sugar; allow mixture to stand 30 minutes as juice collects.

3. Stir in cooled sugar syrup, cream, and vanilla until completely mixed. Chill in refrigerator 2 to 3 hours. Freeze according to ice cream manufacturer's directions.

Makes 1 quart.

MINT CHOCOLATE CRUMB ICE CREAM

Chocolate cookies and refreshing mint make this a favorite flavor for all. If you prefer, omit the green food color; the ice cream will still have the same mint flavor.

    2 eggs
    ⅔ cup sugar
    1 cup milk
    2 cups whipping cream
    2 teaspoons peppermint extract
    ⅛ teaspoon green food color
        (optional)
    1 cup coarsely chopped chocolate
        sandwich cookies (8 to
        10 cookies)

1. In a large microwave-safe bowl, beat eggs and sugar until mixture is thick and lemon colored. Add milk and mix thoroughly. Microwave on medium (50%) until mixture boils and thickens (5 to 7 minutes). Chill in refrigerator about 30 minutes.

2. Stir in cream, peppermint extract, and food color, if desired. Chill in refrigerator 2 to 3 hours. Freeze according to ice cream freezer manufacturer's directions until ice cream is just soft.

3. Fold chopped cookies into soft ice cream. Freeze until firm.

Makes 1 quart.

ROSEMARY'S CREAMY RICE PUDDING

Rosemary's grandmother made a creamy rice pudding that cooks beautifully in the microwave, which eliminates the hour of cooking and stirring necessitated by conventional cooking.

- 1 cup whole milk
- 1 cup long-grain rice
- 1 can (13½ oz) evaporated milk
- 1 tablespoon vanilla extract
- ½ cup sugar
- 1 egg
- ¼ teaspoon ground cinnamon

1. In a 4-quart microwave-safe casserole, combine whole milk and rice. Cover and microwave on high (100%) until milk is absorbed by rice (7 to 9 minutes).

2. Stir in evaporated milk, vanilla, sugar, egg, and cinnamon. Cover and microwave on medium (50%) until rice is tender and liquid is nearly absorbed (8 to 10 minutes). Let stand 5 to 10 minutes; pudding will continue to absorb liquid, and rice will soften. Serve warm or cold.

Serves 6.

BLUEBERRY-LEMON MOUSSE PARFAITS

This pretty layered dessert has a tart, lemony flavor that will be a favorite with guests. Plan to let the mousse chill at least 2 hours in the refrigerator to become firm.

- 1 cup sugar
- ½ cup cornstarch
- 2½ cups milk
- ½ cup lemon juice (about 3 lemons)
- 2 tablespoons grated lemon rind
- 4 egg whites
- 1 cup fresh blueberries, cleaned and drained
  Lemon slices, for garnish

1. In a 3-quart microwave-safe dish, combine ¾ cup of the sugar and the cornstarch. Stir in milk and mix until smooth. Cover and microwave on high (100%) until mixture boils and thickens (5 to 6 minutes), stirring every 2 minutes. Stir in lemon juice and lemon rind. Let cool to room temperature.

2. In a small mixer bowl, combine egg whites and the remaining ¼ cup sugar. Beat until whites form soft peaks. Fold into lemon mixture. Spoon 2 tablespoons of lemon mousse into each of 8 parfait dishes. Spoon 2 tablespoons of the blueberries on top of each. Repeat layers, ending with lemon mousse. Cover and refrigerate at least 2 hours until firm. To serve, garnish with lemon slices.

Serves 8.

MINTED CHOCOLATE-RASPBERRY MOUSSE

Serve this incredibly rich mousse in very small dishes.

- 2 squares (1 oz each) unsweetened chocolate
- 1 can (14 oz) sweetened condensed milk
- 1 teaspoon vanilla extract
- ½ teaspoon peppermint extract
- 1 cup whipping cream, whipped, or 1 container (16 oz) nondairy whipped topping
- 1 container (8 oz) raspberry yogurt
  Fresh mint leaves, for garnish
  Fresh raspberries, for garnish (optional)

1. In a 4-cup microwave-safe measure, microwave chocolate on high (100%) until melted (1 to 2 minutes), stirring twice. Stir in milk, vanilla, and peppermint extract. Microwave on high until chocolate mixture is bubbly (2 to 3 minutes), stirring twice. Let cool completely.

2. Reserve ¼ cup of the whipped cream for garnish. Fold yogurt and the remaining whipped cream into chocolate mixture. Pour into stemmed sherbet dishes and garnish with reserved whipped cream, mint leaves, and raspberries, if used.

Serves 4 to 6.

RICH BUTTERSCOTCH TARTS

The butterscotch filling in these tarts is very sweet. Present them after a light meal of your favorite chicken salad served in radicchio cups.

- ½ cup firmly packed brown sugar
- 2 tablespoons cornstarch
- 1 tablespoon flour
- ¼ teaspoon salt
- 2 cups milk
- 2 eggs, slightly beaten
- 1 tablespoon butter or margarine
- 1 teaspoon vanilla extract
- 4 baked tart shells
  Whipped cream, for garnish (optional)

1. In a 4-cup microwave-safe measure, combine brown sugar, cornstarch, flour, and salt. Stir in milk. Microwave on high (100%) until milk just starts a full boil (6 to 8 minutes), stirring every 2 minutes. Be careful not to overcook.

2. Slowly stir eggs into milk mixture until well combined. Microwave on high until thickened (1 to 2 minutes). Stir in butter and vanilla. Spoon mixture into tart shells. Cover and chill. Serve, topped with whipped cream, if desired.

Serves 4.

*Rich Butterscotch Tarts will
satisfy a dessert lover's craving
for sweets. Garnish them
with whipped cream rosettes and
slivered kumquat zest.*

2. Stir in the water and microwave on high until sauce boils and thickens (3½ to 5 minutes). Add vanilla and stir well. Use immediately or store in refrigerator up to 1 week.

Makes 2 cups.

SINFUL HOT FUDGE

Indulge all your fantasies of hot fudge sundaes with this thick dark chocolate sauce.

    1 can (14 oz) sweetened
       condensed milk
    4 squares (1 oz each)
       unsweetened chocolate
    1 tablespoon butter or
       margarine
    1 teaspoon vanilla extract

In a medium microwave-safe bowl, combine condensed milk and chocolate. Microwave on high (100%) until chocolate is nearly melted (3 to 4 minutes), stirring twice. Stir in butter and vanilla until mixture is smooth and thick. Use immediately or store in refrigerator up to 1 week.

Makes 2 cups.

RIPE STRAWBERRY SAUCE

Ripe strawberries are juicy enough to create this sauce. The strawberry flavor is perfect with Luscious Pound Cake (see page 104) and doubles the pleasure of Fresh Strawberry Ice Cream (see page 97).

    1 cup ripe strawberries,
       washed, hulled, and crushed
    ½ cup water
    1 cup sugar
    2 tablespoons cornstarch

In a 2-quart microwave-safe casserole, stir together all ingredients. Cover and microwave on high (100%) until mixture boils, thickens, and becomes clear (3 to 4 minutes), stirring twice. Microwave again on high until mixture boils 30 seconds. Let cool slightly and use immediately or store in refrigerator up to 3 days.

Makes about 2 cups.

Special Feature

DESSERT SAUCES

Homemade sauces are the perfect accompaniment for special desserts. Use these sauces with cakes such as Luscious Pound Cake (see page 104), ice cream (see page 97), or fresh fruit. All can be served either cold or hot; to reheat, microwave on high (100%) 30 to 60 seconds per cup, stirring once.

PIÑA COLADA SAUCE

Spread this sauce (at bottom in photograph above) on plain cheesecake or serve on pineapple sherbet.

    1 can (12 oz) piña colada mix
    1 tablespoon cornstarch
    1 teaspoon water
    2 tablespoons rum
    ½ cup flaked coconut

In a 4-cup microwave-safe measure, microwave piña colada mix on high (100%) until boiling (4 to 5½ minutes). Combine cornstarch with the water and stir rapidly into hot mix. Microwave on high until slightly thickened (2 to 3 minutes). Stir in rum and coconut. Let cool slightly and use immediately or store in refrigerator up to 1 week.

Makes 2 cups.

RICH VANILLA SAUCE

Reverse the usual and try serving vanilla sauce on chocolate ice cream (see page 97). It is a taste treat on homemade gingerbread (see page 89) or fresh fruit.

    ½ cup butter
    ⅓ cup confectioners' sugar
    3 tablespoons cornstarch
    1½ cups water
    1 tablespoon vanilla extract

1. In a 1½-quart microwave-safe casserole, microwave butter on high (100%) until melted (30 to 60 seconds). Sift sugar and cornstarch into butter; stir until smooth.

FRUIT

Fruit desserts fit readily into today's light and healthy meals.

FRESH PEACH-ALMOND CRUNCH

Other fresh fruits in season, such as pears, nectarines, or apples, may be substituted in this old-fashioned dessert updated for microwave cooking.

- 5 to 6 cups peaches (6 to 8 peaches), peeled and sliced
- ½ teaspoon ground nutmeg
- ½ cup firmly packed dark brown sugar
- ½ cup slivered almonds
- ¼ cup flour
- ¼ cup butter or margarine

1. In a large bowl combine peaches and nutmeg, stirring gently to coat. Spread peaches in an ungreased 8-inch-diameter microwave-safe baking dish.

2. In a small bowl combine brown sugar, slivered almonds, and flour. Cut in butter until mixture is crumbly. Sprinkle over coated peaches.

3. Microwave on high (100%) until peaches are tender and hot (5 to 7 minutes). Serve warm or chilled.

Serves 6.

STUFFED BAKED APPLES

This homey, simple dessert brings images of crisp winter evenings and fresh apples. Select firm cooking apples that will hold their shape during baking.

- 4 medium-sized firm apples
- ¼ cup raisins
- ¼ cup chopped walnuts
- 2 tablespoons sugar
- 1 tablespoon butter or margarine

1. Wash apples; remove core from each without cutting through bottom of apple. Stand cored apples in a 9-inch-diameter microwave-safe baking dish.

2. In a small bowl combine raisins, walnuts, and sugar. Add butter; cream mixture together. Divide stuffing evenly among apples, filling center cavity of each.

3. Microwave apples on high (100%) until apples are tender when pierced with a fork (9 to 11 minutes). Let stand 5 minutes. Serve warm.

Serves 4.

SCANDINAVIAN FRUIT SOUP

Scandinavian cooks use dried fruit to concoct a most intriguing soup that they serve for dessert. It is a surprise on any menu.

- 1 package (6 oz) pitted prunes
- 1 package (6 oz) dried apricot halves or mixed dried fruit
- ½ cup raisins
- 2 tart cooking apples, peeled, cored, and cut into ¾-inch chunks
- 2 cinnamon sticks (2 in. each)
- 2 cups water, plus 1 tablespoon water
- ½ cup honey
- 2 tablespoons cornstarch
  Whipped cream, for garnish
  Ground cinnamon, for sprinkling

1. In a 3-quart microwave-safe casserole, combine prunes, apricots, raisins, apples, and cinnamon sticks. In a small container stir together the 2 cups water and honey; add to fruits, stirring to combine.

2. Cover and microwave on high (100%) until dried fruits are plump and apples are crisp-tender (6 to 8 minutes).

3. In a small bowl combine cornstarch and the 1 tablespoon water until smooth. Stir rapidly into fruit mixture until well blended. Cover and microwave on high until liquid is thickened (2 to 4 minutes). Serve hot or cold in soup bowls, garnished with whipped cream and sprinkled with cinnamon.

Makes 3 to 4 cups, serves 4 to 6.

APPLE-CRANBERRY CRISP

This festive and colorful dessert is a special treat during the fall when fresh apples and cranberries are readily available. Try it for a change-of-pace Thanksgiving dessert.

- 4 cups sliced apples (about 4 medium apples)
- 1½ cups fresh cranberries
- 1 cup granulated sugar
- ¾ cup firmly packed brown sugar
- ½ cup whole wheat flour
- ½ cup oatmeal
- 1 teaspoon ground cinnamon
- ½ cup butter or margarine

1. In an ungreased 9-inch-diameter microwave-safe baking dish, combine apples, cranberries, and granulated sugar; stir to blend.

2. In a large bowl combine brown sugar, flour, oatmeal, and cinnamon. Cut in butter until mixture is crumbly. Sprinkle flour mixture evenly over apple mixture.

3. Microwave on high (100%) until fruits are tender (12 to 14 minutes). Let stand 10 minutes before serving.

Serves 6 to 8.

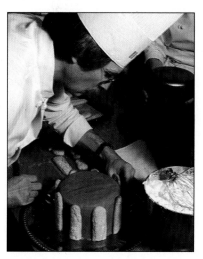

The soft pink cast of Cranberry-Poached Pears makes them a picture-perfect dessert. Garnish them with sprigs of fresh mint.

CRANBERRY-POACHED PEARS

Cranberry juice gives a soft pink hue to these pears. Served in individual crystal dishes, they are an elegant finish to a special meal. The pears are delicious served warm or chilled.

> 4 medium pears, stems attached
> 1 bottle (32 oz) cranberry juice cocktail
> 2 tablespoons cornstarch
> Fresh mint or lemon leaves, for garnish

1. Peel each pear, leaving stem in place. Remove core by cutting up from bottom of pear, stopping just short of the stem.

2. Place cored pears in a 4-quart microwave-safe casserole and pour cranberry juice over them. Cover and microwave on high (100%) until pears are tender when pierced carefully with a toothpick (14 to 18 minutes), turning pears over twice in juice so color is evenly distributed. With a slotted spoon remove pears, reserving hot juice; set pears aside.

3. Pour 1 cup of the reserved hot juice into a 2-cup microwave-safe measure. In a small container combine cornstarch with an additional ¼ cup of the reserved hot juice, then rapidly stir cornstarch mixture into the 1 cup hot juice. Microwave cornstarch–hot juice mixture on high 1 minute. Stir, then microwave again on high until juice thickens and is clear (1 to 2½ minutes).

4. To serve, place a pear in each individual serving dish. Spoon warm sauce over pears and garnish with mint leaves.

Serves 4.

---

menu

VALENTINE DESSERT PARTY BUFFET

Chocolate Crumb Cheesecake

Luscious Pound Cake

Flaming Cherries Jubilee

Rich Vanilla Ice Cream (see page 97)

Fresh Fruit Bowl

Pastel Mints

Hot Coffee and Tea

A special day for lovers is the perfect occasion to celebrate with a party of just desserts for six to eight close friends. Set the buffet table with a pretty lace cloth; use frilly napkins and fresh flowers. Bring out your silver and antique serving pieces. Your friends will love the excuse to sample the sweets, so this selection includes some rich treats. But it also includes desserts for those whose tastes are more restrained, such as a bowl of fresh fruit. Just cut up and combine three or four of the freshest fruits in season to serve on the pound cake or alone.

CHOCOLATE CRUMB CHEESECAKE

This rich confection will appeal to chocolate and cheesecake lovers alike. It is elegant presented on a footed silver serving dish. Make this dessert in the morning and refrigerate so it will be thoroughly chilled and firm by party time.

> 11 ounces cream cheese
> 1 egg
> ⅔ cup sugar
> 1 teaspoon vanilla extract
> 1 cup chocolate sandwich cookie crumbs (about 12 cookies), for sprinkling

1. In a large microwave-safe mixing bowl, microwave cream cheese on high (100%) until softened (30 to 60 seconds). With electric mixer cream the cheese until smooth. Add egg and beat until well combined. Add ⅓ cup of the sugar and beat well. Add the remaining ⅓ cup sugar and the vanilla and beat until well combined.

2. Pour mixture into an ungreased 8-inch-diameter microwave-safe pie plate. Microwave on medium (50%) until outside edges of cake begin to solidify (3 to 5 minutes). With a rubber spatula stir outside edges of cake to center of dish and smooth top. Microwave on medium until center is soft and edges are firm (3 to 4 minutes).

3. Sprinkle cake with cookie crumbs, covering cake completely. Microwave on medium until only slightly soft (2 to 4 minutes). Refrigerate at least 2 hours before serving; cheesecake will firm as it cools.

Serves 6 to 8.

LUSCIOUS POUND CAKE

This rich pound cake is delicious topped with Flaming Cherries Jubilee (recipe at right) or an assortment of sparkling fresh berries. Try the left-over pound cake with your choice of a homemade dessert sauce (see page 100). The Ripe Strawberry Sauce is especially good on this rich cake.

- 1 tablespoon granulated sugar, for sprinkling
- 1½ cups butter
- 1 box (16 oz) confectioners' sugar, plus confectioners' sugar for dusting (optional)
- 6 eggs
- 1 teaspoon vanilla extract
- 2½ cups sifted flour

1. Generously grease a 12-cup micro-wave-safe bundt cake dish and sprinkle with granulated sugar; set aside. In a large microwave-safe mixing bowl, microwave butter on medium (50%) until softened (1 to 1½ minutes). Beat in the 1 box confectioners' sugar until mixture is fluffy. Add eggs one at a time, beating until well blended. Beat in vanilla. Fold in flour until mixture is smooth and well combined.

2. Pour batter into prepared dish, making sure surface of batter is smooth and even. Microwave cake on medium 12 minutes, rotating dish twice. Then microwave on medium-high (70%) until top of cake appears dry and surface bubbles break (6 to 8 minutes).

3. Let cake cool directly on heatproof surface 15 minutes. Invert cake on a serving plate and let cool completely. Dust top with confectioners' sugar, if desired.

Serves 10 to 12.

FLAMING CHERRIES JUBILEE

This flaming sauce is a showstopper and an elegant topping for Luscious Pound Cake (recipe at left) or Rich Vanilla Ice Cream (see page 97). Be sure to use a heat-resistant glass measuring cup to warm the brandy in the microwave before lighting it. Warming the brandy makes it easier to ignite.

- 2 cans (16 oz each) pitted dark sweet cherries, undrained
- ¼ cup currant jelly
- 1 tablespoon lemon juice
- 2 tablespoons cornstarch
- ⅓ cup cherry brandy, plus 2 tablespoons cherry brandy, to ignite over cherries

1. Drain cherries, reserving 1 cup of the juice. In a 2-quart microwave-safe casserole, combine reserved juice and jelly. Cover and microwave on high (100%) until mixture is boiling (3 to 4 minutes). Add cherries, stir to combine, and microwave on high until cherry mixture is hot (2 to 4 minutes).

2. In a custard cup combine lemon juice and cornstarch until well blended and lump-free; then stir into hot cherry mixture. Microwave on high until mixture boils and thickens (3 to 5 minutes). Add the ⅓ cup cherry brandy and stir until well combined. Pour brandy mixture into chafing dish.

3. Place the 2 tablespoons cherry brandy in a 1-cup heat-resistant glass measure. Microwave on high until brandy is hot (30 to 45 seconds). With a long match, *carefully* ignite brandy; *using great caution,* pour flaming brandy over cherries. Allow flame to burn out before serving. Ladle brandied cherries over pound cake or ice cream and serve.

Makes 3 cups, serves 6 to 8.

Choose from this sumptuous Valentine's buffet, which includes rich chocolate-topped cheesecake and Flaming Cherries Jubilee atop Luscious Pound Cake.

Tuck Toasted Peanut Clusters (see page 108) into an attractive box for a delightful gift that belies its simple preparation and ingredients.

Gifts From the Microwave

To celebrate a holiday or birthday, welcome a new baby or a new neighbor, or thank a hostess or a friend, food gifts are always welcome. Take advantage of nature's bounty and the microwave oven to prepare Midwestern Corn Relish (see page 119), Fresh Herb Vinegars (see page 118), and Spicy Citrus Jelly (see page 120) when fruits and vegetables are ripe. A microwave oven can shorten the time you need to prepare them, and microwave gifts are easy for children to make and give with pride of accomplishment. Many of these recipes can be made ahead, so you can stock the pantry shelves with a delicious selection of perfect treats for gift giving.

SWEETS

A gift of sweet morsels is appropriate for anyone on your gift list. For cooks and children who enjoy baking, including a recipe card is sure to be appreciated.

SHORTBREAD COOKIE TAGS

Try cutting shapes with cookie cutters—hearts for a valentine, animals to tie on a child's gift, or the silhouette of a brother's favorite vehicle for an unbirthday treat. Ice the cookie tags with Royal Decorator Frosting, which hardens as it stands so it won't smear. You may want to tint it with food color to achieve special effects. Be sure to keep the frosting covered until you are ready to use it, since it dries quickly. The frosting recipe may be doubled or tripled. Extra frosting may be frozen in tightly covered containers.

> ½ pound butter, softened (see page 87)
> 1¼ cups confectioners' sugar
> ½ teaspoon vanilla extract
> 1 tablespoon sour cream
> 2¾ cups flour

Royal Decorator Frosting

> 1 egg white
> 1 cup confectioners' sugar
> ¼ teaspoon cream of tartar
> Food color (optional)

1. In a large mixing bowl, combine butter and confectioners' sugar until fluffy. Stir in vanilla and sour cream. Add flour ½ cup at a time. Dough will be stiff. Chill dough in freezer 10 minutes.

2. On a floured surface, roll dough into a ¼-inch-thick rectangle. With a pastry cutter or knife, cut dough into 1- by 3-inch rectangles. With a skewer pierce each rectangle in center of a short side.

3. Place a paper towel on a 12-inch-diameter microwave-safe plate. Arrange 6 to 8 pierced rectangles in a circle on paper towel. Microwave on medium (50%) until tops appear dry (3 to 4 minutes). Remove from plate and cool on a wire rack. Repeat with remaining pierced rectangles. Ice with Royal Decorator Frosting.

Makes about 30 cookie tags.

Royal Decorator Frosting In a medium bowl combine egg white, confectioners' sugar, and cream of tartar. Beat with electric mixer until mixture is thick and stiff peaks form (about 8 minutes). Cover bowl with a damp towel until you are ready to use icing. To tint icing, transfer small amounts to separate dishes and add a few drops of food color, if desired.

Makes about ¾ cup.

MAPLE-WALNUT ICE CREAM SYRUP

Ice cream sundae lovers will be thrilled to receive a jar of your homemade topping. For microwave users attach a label with instructions to reheat by microwaving on high (100%) until warm (1 to 1½ minutes). If you anticipate that the topping will be stored longer than 2 months, place syrup in sterilized jars and process in a boiling water bath (see page 122).

> 1 cup light corn syrup
> 1 cup maple syrup
> ½ cup sugar
> 2 cups coarsely chopped walnut pieces

1. Sterilize jars if using a boiling water bath. Meanwhile in a 3-quart microwave-safe casserole, combine corn syrup, maple syrup, and sugar. Microwave on high (100%) until mixture boils (4 to 6 minutes), stirring once. Stir in walnuts and microwave on high until walnut mixture boils again (2 to 3 minutes).

2. Reduce power to medium (50%) and boil maple-walnut syrup 1 to 2 minutes. Transfer syrup to a clean container, cover tightly, and store in refrigerator. Syrup will keep refrigerated up to 2 months. For longer storage, ladle syrup into ½-pint canning jars to within ½ inch of rims. Process jars 10 minutes in a boiling water bath.

Makes 4 half-pints.

TOASTED PEANUT CLUSTERS

The winning combination of chocolate and peanuts is further enhanced by butterscotch in this easy-to-make candy that tastes simply delicious!

> 2 cups salted peanuts
> 1 package (12 oz) semisweet chocolate chips
> 1 package (6 oz) butterscotch chips

1. Spread single layer of peanuts in the bottom of a shallow microwave-safe baking dish. Microwave on high (100%) until peanuts are toasted (3 to 5 minutes), stirring every minute and watching carefully to prevent nuts from burning. Set toasted peanuts aside.

2. In a 4-cup microwave-safe measure, combine chocolate and butterscotch chips. Microwave on high until chips are melted (2 to 3 minutes), stirring twice.

3. Add toasted peanuts to chocolate mixture and stir until thoroughly combined. Using a teaspoon, drop toasted peanut mixture into clusters on a sheet of waxed paper. Let cool until solid (about 15 minutes). Store in refrigerator.

Makes 3 dozen clusters.

Edible Shortbread Cookie Tags cut into whimsical shapes and trimmed with frosting are a unique treat to tie on a gift for a special person.

For a gift whose memory will linger, make Elegant Chocolate Cups with white chocolate and fill each with a Fancy Truffle (both recipes on page 111) coated with cocoa or chocolate sprinkles.

ICED PRETZELS

These treats are sold in the fanciest candy shops, but you can easily make them at home. Take a tip from the candy shops and try dipping thick potato chips, dried fruits, rice cereal, or chocolate sandwich cookies in the melted chocolate.

> 1 bar (8 oz) white or milk chocolate candy
> 1 bag (8 oz) small pretzel rings

1. Place candy in a 2-cup microwave-safe measure. Microwave on high (100%) until chocolate is shiny (1 to 2½ minutes), stirring every 30 seconds. Stir until very smooth.

2. Set a wire rack on a tray. Using two forks or chopsticks, dip pretzels into melted chocolate, then place on wire rack to cool. Excess chocolate can be removed from tray, added to measuring cup, and reheated on medium (50%) until thin and smooth enough for dipping (30 to 60 seconds). Store coated pretzels tightly covered in refrigerator. They will keep refrigerated up to 1 month.

Makes about 5 dozen small pretzel rings.

ELEGANT CHOCOLATE CUPS

Use chocolate cups to serve rich Minted Chocolate-Raspberry Mousse (see page 98), liqueurs, or homemade ice cream (see page 97) for a special occasion. You can also make the cups with white chocolate and place a truffle in each (see recipe at right), then pack them in a fancy box to create an exquisite sweet gift.

> 3 squares (1 oz each) semisweet
>   or white chocolate
> 2 teaspoons shortening

1. Place chocolate and shortening in a 2-cup microwave-safe measure. Microwave on high (100%) until chocolate is shiny (1 to 2½ minutes for dark chocolate, 2 to 3 minutes for white chocolate), stirring every 30 seconds. Stir until very smooth.

2. Use miniature foil or paper candy cups. (If using paper, double the cups to provide needed support.) Pour about 1 teaspoon of the melted chocolate into each cup, turning cup and using back of a teaspoon to evenly coat bottom and sides of cup. Refrigerate until firm (at least 2 hours). Transfer to an airtight container and store in refrigerator. Chocolate cups will keep refrigerated about 1 month.

Makes 16 to 18 cups.

BRANDIED CITRUS PINEAPPLE

Arranged in a decorative jar, these pineapple spears and orange slices make an attractive gift. Serve this treat with baked ham or add it to a festive fruit bowl.

> 1 large ripe pineapple
> ½ cup sugar
> ½ cup pineapple juice
> ½ cup water
> 1 small orange (unpeeled),
>   thinly sliced
> 2 tablespoons brandy

1. Cut off leafy crown of pineapple and quarter fruit. Remove and discard core; cut fruit into spears that will stand up in a pint jar.

2. In a 3-quart microwave-safe casserole, combine sugar, pineapple juice, and the water. Cover and microwave on high (100%) until liquid boils (3 to 5 minutes), stirring once. Add pineapple spears and orange slices. Microwave on high until mixture boils (3 to 5 minutes). Stir, then microwave again on high until mixture boils 1 minute.

3. Divide pineapple spears and orange slices equally into 2 pint jars with lids. Add 1 tablespoon brandy to each jar. Pour hot liquid over spears to cover completely. Cover and store in refrigerator. Brandied fruit will keep refrigerated up to 3 months.

Makes 2 pints.

PUMPKIN-NUT RING

Decorate this cake for a holiday gift with maraschino cherries and green frosting leaves or real holly leaves.

> 1 cup chopped walnuts
> 2½ teaspoons ground cinnamon
> ½ cup milk
> 1½ teaspoons lemon juice
> 1 cup sugar
> 1 cup cooked pumpkin
> ⅓ cup vegetable oil
> 2 eggs
> 1⅔ cups flour
> 1 teaspoon baking soda
> ½ teaspoon salt
> ½ teaspoon ground nutmeg

1. Generously grease a 6-cup microwave-safe ring mold with shortening. Evenly sprinkle ¼ cup of the walnuts on bottom of mold. Sprinkle 1 teaspoon of the cinnamon over nuts. Set aside.

2. In a large mixing bowl, combine milk and lemon juice; let stand until milk sours (about 5 minutes). Add sugar, pumpkin, oil, and eggs; mix well. Add flour, baking soda, salt, nutmeg, and the remaining ¾ cup walnuts and 1½ teaspoons cinnamon. Beat until well blended (about 2 minutes).

3. Pour mixture into prepared ring mold. Microwave on medium-high (70%) until cake loosens from sides of mold (14 to 16 minutes).

4. Let stand directly on heatproof surface 5 minutes. Invert cake onto serving tray and let cool completely.

Serves 6 to 8.

FANCY TRUFFLES

Children love rolling truffles into balls and adding fancy coatings. Let them make a box of these for grandma, a favorite uncle, or their teacher. Include a note that the truffles should be stored in the refrigerator.

> 8 squares (1 oz each) semisweet
>   chocolate
> 1 bar (8 oz) milk chocolate
> 2 tablespoons butter
> 1¼ cups sifted confectioners'
>   sugar
> 1 teaspoon vanilla extract
>   Coatings, such as
>   confectioners' sugar, cocoa,
>   ground nuts, colored
>   sprinkles, crushed chocolate
>   cookies, flaked coconut

1. In a 2-quart microwave-safe casserole, combine chocolates and butter. Microwave on high (100%) until mixture is just melted (3 to 4 minutes), stirring every minute. Stir until smooth. Let cool 10 minutes.

2. Beat in the 1¼ cups confectioners' sugar and vanilla. Chill chocolate mixture in refrigerator until mixture is firm enough to hold a shape (about 30 minutes).

3. To make each truffle, roll 1 to 2 teaspoonfuls chocolate mixture into a ball. Roll balls in your choice of coatings. Place truffles on a tray and chill until firm (15 to 20 minutes), then place truffles in an airtight container and store in refrigerator.

Makes about 3 dozen truffles.

... ON PACKING FOR MAILING

Your food gifts will be appreciated by friends and family away from home if you take the time to pack them properly, ensuring safe arrival. These suggestions will help.

☐ Select foods that can withstand packing and handling. Candy, bar cookies, nuts, and dense cakes are all good candidates.

☐ Pack all food in sturdy containers that will not break in transit. Metal tins and boxes, plastic containers, and heavy cardboard boxes all ship well.

☐ To preserve freshness, enclose individual items in plastic wrap as soon as they cool. Place nuts in sealable plastic bags. Mail as quickly as possible.

☐ Select a mailing carton that is just slightly larger than the food container it will hold. Pad food container on all sides with crumpled or shredded newspaper or plastic foam packing material. Plain unbuttered popcorn is also an effective cushion.

☐ Be sure to tape a duplicate address label directly on the carton before wrapping it. Then wrap carton in sturdy paper and secure with reinforced tape. Write address label with a permanent marker (deliveries are made in all weather) and clearly label the package: *food— perishable.*

☐ Have package weighed and sent by the post office or a package delivery service.

ROCKY ROAD FUDGE ROLL

This candy roll looks delicious sliced and included in a candy assortment.

> 1 bar (8 oz) milk chocolate
> ¾ cup coarsely chopped walnuts
> 1 cup miniature marshmallows
> ½ cup crushed chocolate sandwich cookies

1. In a 4-cup microwave-safe measure, break chocolate into pieces. Microwave on high (100%) until chocolate is melted (2 to 4 minutes), stirring twice.

2. Stir in walnuts, marshmallows, and crushed cookies. Let stand 15 minutes.

3. Scrape mixture onto sheet of aluminum foil. Shape into 2-inch-diameter roll and wrap in foil. Refrigerate until solid.

4. To give as a gift, wrap entire roll in plastic wrap and tie with ribbons. Include instructions to keep roll refrigerated until used and to cut roll into ¼-inch-thick slices to serve.

Makes one 12-inch-long roll, about 40 slices.

PICKLES AND PRESERVES

Stock your pantry shelves with crisp pickles and tasty preserves. If you plan to give pickled foods as gifts, just remember to allow time for the pickling to be completed.

JALAPEÑO CHILE CHEESE

Pack this tangy cheese into a decorative crock and serve it with crisp crackers as an appetizer or snack.

> 1 pound sharp Cheddar cheese, grated
> 1 package (3 oz) cream cheese
> ½ cup butter or margarine
> 1 tablespoon finely chopped onion
> 2 to 3 tablespoons chopped jalapeño chile, or to taste
> ½ teaspoon paprika
> 1 to 2 tablespoons butter (optional)

1. Place Cheddar cheese in a medium microwave-safe mixing bowl. Add cream cheese and the ½ cup butter. Microwave on medium-low (30%) until cheeses are softened but not melted (1 to 3 minutes), stirring twice. It is important that cheeses do not melt; stirring will distribute heat and help to soften cheeses without melting them.

2. Place softened cheese mixture in work bowl of food processor. Add onion, jalapeño chile, and paprika. Process cheese mixture until evenly blended. Scoop mixture into a decorative crock, cover, and store in refrigerator.

3. Cheese will keep refrigerated up to 2 weeks. If storage up to 2 months is desired, in a small microwave-safe measure, microwave the remaining butter on high (100%) 30 to 60 seconds. Pour melted butter over cheese in crock, covering cheese completely to seal. Refrigerate.

Makes 1½ cups.

PICKLED CARROT STICKS

Take these delicious pickled carrots to a family picnic.

- 2 or 3 medium carrots
- ¼ cup water
- ½ cup cider vinegar
- ⅓ cup sugar
- ½ teaspoon salt
- 1½ teaspoons pickling spice
- 1 cinnamon stick (2 in. long)

1. Wash and peel carrots. Cut into sticks about 3½ inches long and about the thickness of a pencil.

2. In a 1½-quart microwave-safe casserole, place carrot sticks and the water. Cover and microwave on high (100%) until carrot sticks are crisp-tender (3 to 4 minutes), stirring once. Rinse immediately with cold tap water until cool. Drain. Pack tightly into a clean pint jar and set aside.

3. In a 2-cup microwave-safe measure, combine vinegar, sugar, salt, pickling spice, and cinnamon stick. Microwave on high until mixture boils (1 to 2 minutes), stirring once. Pour hot mixture over carrot sticks, inserting cinnamon stick in center of jar. Cover and refrigerate at least 1 week before serving. Store in refrigerator. Pickled carrots keep refrigerated up to 2 months.

Makes 1 pint.

PICKLED OLIVES

Pack these olives in decorative jars for gift giving. Make them ahead, since they are better if they marinate a week before being served. The olives will keep refrigerated for up to 6 months. They are a delicious cocktail nibble and a tasty addition to an antipasto platter.

- 2 cans (16 oz) pitted green olives
- 1 cup olive oil
- ½ cup red wine vinegar
- 2 tablespoons pickling spice
- 2 to 3 drops hot-pepper sauce

1. Drain olives, discarding liquid. Place olives in a clean 1-quart glass jar with lid.

2. In a 4-cup microwave-safe measure, combine oil, vinegar, pickling spice, and hot-pepper sauce. Microwave on high (100%) until mixture begins to simmer around outside edges (2 to 3 minutes). Let stand 5 minutes, then pour mixture over olives. Cover tightly. Let olives stand at room temperature at least 24 hours, shaking jar several times.

3. With a slotted spoon, remove marinated olives from pickling liquid and pack them in decorative glass containers with lids. Fill each container almost to the top with pickling liquid. Cover and label containers; store in refrigerator.

Makes 3 cups.

Get into the holiday spirit and prepare these fudge rolls ahead for Christmas gifts. They are fun for children to make and give to their friends.

Arrange carrots, whole mushrooms, strips of red bell pepper, and perfect florets of broccoli and cauliflower in layers in a clear glass jar; the contrasting colors will be visible as the vegetables sparkle in the brine. Italian Marinated Vegetables will darken somewhat during aging, but their flavors will not be affected.

CUMBERLAND SAUCE

This English sauce is often brushed on chicken or beef during roasting. Store it in the refrigerator or, for long storage, place it in sterilized jars and process in a boiling water bath (see page 122).

- 1 jar (12 oz) red currant jelly
- ¼ cup Cointreau or orange-flavored liqueur
- 2 teaspoons brown mustard
- 1 small onion, finely chopped
Zest of 1 orange, cut into thin strips

1. Sterilize jars if using a boiling water bath. Meanwhile in a 4-cup microwave-safe measure, combine jelly, Cointreau, mustard, and onion. Microwave on high (100%) until jelly melts (2 to 3 minutes). Stir in zest.

2. Cool sauce and pour into half-pint jars. Cover tightly and store in refrigerator. The sauce will keep refrigerated up to 1 month. For longer storage, process 10 minutes in a boiling water bath.

Makes 2 half-pints.

ITALIAN MARINATED VEGETABLES

You will find these vegetables labeled *giardiniera* in Italian delicatessens. Prepare them yourself when summer's bounty is full. Look for a large widemouthed clear glass jar, so the beauty of the vegetables can be seen easily. They will keep refrigerated about 2 months.

    2 cups red wine vinegar
    ½ cup olive oil
    2 tablespoons sugar
    2 tablespoons chopped parsley
    1 teaspoon salt
    3 teaspoons chopped fresh basil
      or 1 teaspoon dried basil
    1½ teaspoons fresh oregano or
      ½ teaspoon dried oregano
    ½ teaspoon freshly ground
      pepper
    2 cloves garlic, minced
    1 medium head broccoli,
      washed and cut into florets
      (about 2½ cups florets)
    1 small cauliflower, washed
      and cut into florets (about
      2½ cups florets)
    1 large carrot, washed, scraped,
      and cut into ½-inch pieces
    1 red bell pepper, cored, seeded,
      and cut into 1-inch pieces
    1 cup small whole mushrooms,
      cleaned
    2 tablespoons lemon juice

1. In a 4-quart microwave-safe casserole, combine vinegar, oil, sugar, parsley, salt, basil, oregano, ground pepper, and garlic. Microwave on high (100%) until mixture boils (4 to 6 minutes).

2. Add broccoli, cauliflower, and carrot. Microwave on high 3 to 4 minutes. Add bell pepper and mushrooms and microwave on high until all vegetables are crisp-tender (2 to 3 minutes). Cool mixture to room temperature, then stir in lemon juice. Pour into a 2-quart glass jar, cover, and refrigerate.

Makes 2 quarts.

Special Note

ELEGANT PRESENTATIONS

Give some thought to packaging your food gift attractively. Gourmet shops are adept at making their food gifts look special. You can use their ideas or any of these suggestions.

☐ Look in gift shops, antique stores, and even second hand shops for attractive food containers. Import shops, discount stores, and the local five-and-dime may all be good sources: Look for containers made of glass, plastic, paper, tin, and cardboard.

☐ Check the fine china department clearance rack for single wine goblets, water glasses, and tumblers from discontinued lines or broken sets. These pieces look quite elegant filled with jellies, jams, and relishes. Olives look terrific in a champagne flute!

☐ Package your gift in a basket or decorated bag with all the ingredients needed to complete a meal. For example, with your spaghetti sauce give a package of pasta, a loaf of Italian bread, and a bottle of wine.

☐ Match the proper serving dish to the food gift you have prepared and give them as a set. A jelly dish with a jar of jelly, a handsome decanter with your liqueur, a holiday tray for cheese or breads, and a hand-decorated basket for serving muffins will all multiply the usefulness of your gift.

☐ Confectioners' waxed tissue paper is available in pretty colors at specialty shops. The waxed surface sheds grease marks.

☐ Place candies in individual bonbon papers. Available in colors, foils, and holiday designs, they add distinction to a box of candy.

☐ If the recipient is also a microwave cook, package the food in a microwave-safe container and label it for microwave reheating.

☐ Lacy paper doilies in a variety of sizes and shapes can be used under food or as a cover for a lid. Tie the doily over the lid with a colorful ribbon.

☐ Wrap your gift in pretty wrapping paper and tie it with lots of ribbon, bows, and streamers for a festive look.

FRUIT LEATHER

Fruit leather can be made with many fruits, including peaches, pears, apples, strawberries, and raspberries. These photographs use peaches to illustrate the process (see recipe for Peach Leather, at right).

1. *Microwave 2 or 3 peaches at a time on high (100%) 15 to 20 seconds so skins slip off easily when peaches are peeled.*

2. *Cut peeled peaches into chunks, drop into work bowl of food processor, and process until smooth (5 to 10 seconds).*

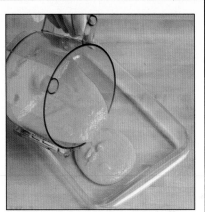

3. *Pour purée into 3-quart shallow microwave-safe baking dish and microwave on medium-low (30%) 45 minutes, stirring every 15 minutes. Then microwave on low (10%) until purée is very thick (50 to 60 minutes), stirring every 15 minutes.*

4. *Pour cooked purée onto aluminum foil–lined cookie sheet, spreading very thin.*

5. *Let stand until purée can be lifted and pulled from foil in a solid sheet. Cut sheet of stiffened purée into 4-inch-square pieces. Roll each piece into a cylinder.*

PEACH LEATHER

Prepare fruit leather (following Step-by-Step at left) when the weather is hot and dry to shorten the drying time of the purée. Although drying time varies with weather conditions, it should be between 24 and 48 hours. Using sweet ripe peaches should eliminate the need for sugar. If you want to add sugar or honey, do so sparingly since flavors concentrate during drying. Experiment with other fruits in season, such as strawberries, pears, apples, or raspberries.

1 quart peaches (4 to 5 lb)

1. Place 2 or 3 peaches in microwave at a time and microwave on high (100%) 15 to 20 seconds so skins slip off easily as fruit is peeled.

2. Peel peaches and cut fruit into chunks. Purée in work bowl of food processor until smooth (5 to 10 seconds). If adding sugar or honey, blend in. Pour purée into a 3-quart shallow microwave-safe baking dish. Microwave on medium-low (30%) 45 minutes, stirring every 15 minutes. Then microwave on low (10%) until purée is very thick (50 to 60 minutes), stirring every 15 minutes.

3. Cover cookie sheet with aluminum foil. Pour cooked purée onto foil, spreading very thin. Let stand until purée can be lifted and pulled away from foil in a solid sheet.

4. Cut sheet of stiffened purée into 4-inch-square pieces. Roll each piece into a cylinder. Enclose each cylinder individually in plastic wrap and store in the refrigerator or freezer; fruit leather will keep refrigerated up to 1 month and frozen up to 1 year.

Makes twelve to fourteen 4-inch-long cylinders.

SPICY PICNIC MUSTARD

Homemade mustard perks up the sandwich board. Spoon it into a decorative crock or mustard pot and add a fresh loaf of dark bread for a tasty gift.

 1 cup white vinegar
 1 cup dry mustard
 ½ teaspoon dried thyme
 3 to 5 drops hot-pepper sauce
 2 eggs, beaten
 ½ cup firmly packed brown sugar

1. In a small bowl combine vinegar, mustard, thyme, and hot-pepper sauce. Let stand 6 hours or overnight.

2. In a 2-quart microwave-safe casserole, combine eggs, brown sugar, and mustard mixture. Microwave on high (100%) until warm (1 minute), stirring twice. Microwave on medium (50%) until mixture thickens and coats a spoon (3 to 4 minutes). Let cool; then spoon into mustard pot or jar, cover, and store in refrigerator. Mustard will keep refrigerated up to 1 month.

Makes 2 cups.

When you've been invited for a weekend at a friend's beach house, bring a crock of homemade mustard, a loaf of hearty bread, a jug of wine, and a whole salami in a picnic basket for a gift that is sure to be appreciated.

117

CHUNKY APPLE-BERRY RELISH

This tart, chunky relish is a delicious accompaniment to chicken, turkey, or pork. For a sparkling gift, present it freshly made in a crystal relish dish with its own spoon. The relish keeps in the refrigerator for 3 days; to store it longer, process 10 minutes in a boiling water bath (see page 122).

- 1 cup fresh cranberries
- ½ cup apple juice
- 2 tablespoons sugar
- ¼ teaspoon each *ground nutmeg and ground allspice*
- 2 *Granny Smith apples, peeled, cored, and cut into ½-inch chunks*

1. Sterilize jar if using a boiling water bath. Meanwhile, in a 2-quart microwave-safe casserole, stir together cranberries, apple juice, sugar, nutmeg, and allspice. Cover and microwave on high (100%) until at least half the cranberries have popped open (3 to 4 minutes), stirring once.

2. Stir in apples and microwave on high until apples are soft enough to crush (3½ to 4½ minutes), stirring once. Crush apples lightly with the back of a spoon, leaving some apple chunks whole. Chill in refrigerator. Serve cold.

Makes about 1½ cups.

Special Feature

FRESH HERB VINEGARS

Herb vinegars are popular food gift suggestions at gourmet stores. They are simple to prepare at home for a fraction of the cost. Packaging is an important part of their presentation, so be sure to collect an interesting assortment of decorative bottles for gift-giving. Always place a fresh herb sprig in each bottle before you fill it with vinegar, and attach a hand-lettered tag with the herb vinegar recipe on each bottle.

Heating the vinegar in the microwave speeds the herb infusion. Some herbs that are especially suitable for infusing vinegar are tarragon, dill, rosemary, thyme, and basil. Purple basil imparts a lovely rose color to the vinegar during the infusion. Be sure to include some sprigs of fresh green basil with the purple, since it is more highly flavored.

- 4 cups white vinegar
- 1 cup coarsely chopped fresh herbs or ½ cup dried herbs

1. Pour vinegar into a 2-quart microwave-safe casserole. Cover and microwave on high (100%) until vinegar is hot (3 to 5 minutes). Place herbs in a clean 1-quart glass jar and pour hot vinegar over them. Cover and let stand in a warm, sunny spot 2 weeks before bottling.

2. When vinegar is ready to be bottled, wash individual bottles and place in each bottle fresh herb sprigs of same herb used in vinegar. Strain infused vinegar to remove old herbs and pour over sprigs in bottles. Cap or cork to seal, then label.

Makes 1 quart.

MIDWESTERN CORN RELISH

The bright colors and nippy taste of this relish make it a perfect accompaniment to beef and pork entrées. For long storage, place the relish in sterilized jars and process in a boiling water bath (see page 122).

    ¼ cup sugar
    1½ teaspoons cornstarch
    1 tablespoon finely chopped
      onion
    2 teaspoons mustard seed
    ¼ teaspoon celery seed
    ⅛ teaspoon ground turmeric
    ¼ cup white vinegar
    3 tablespoons hot water
    2 tablespoons finely chopped
      pimiento
    1½ cups whole corn kernels
      (see Note)

1. Sterilize jars if using a boiling water bath. Meanwhile in a 3-quart microwave-safe casserole, combine sugar, cornstarch, onion, mustard seed, celery seed, and turmeric. Gradually stir in vinegar and the water, mixing well.

2. Cover and microwave on high (100%) until hot (5 to 7 minutes). Stir well, then add pimiento and corn. Cover and microwave on high until mixture boils and thickens.

3. Ladle relish into clean jars or other containers with lids. Cover and store in refrigerator. Relish keeps refrigerated 4 to 6 weeks. For longer storage, process 10 minutes in a boiling water bath.

Makes 3 half-pints.

Note If using frozen corn, microwave on high 3 minutes before adding to recipe. If using canned corn, drain very well.

Step-by-Step

DRYING HERBS IN THE MICROWAVE

If you grow herbs or have friends with extra herbs, dry the herbs in the microwave. You will be surprised by the brilliant colors they retain. Follow these directions for drying. When you give the dried herbs as a gift, attach instructions to store them in a cool, dark place.

1. *Pick fresh herbs during midday when flavors are intense and foliage dry. Good candidates for drying include basil, parsley, mint, sage, thyme, and oregano. If necessary, wash and dry herbs thoroughly.*

2. *Remove leaves from stems and place leaves in a single layer on a paper towel. Do not overcrowd.*

3. *For best results microwave a small batch of leaves at a time. Microwave on high (100%) until leaves are dry and crisp. Time will depend on type and amount of herb to be dried. Begin microwaving 2 to 3 minutes and add time in 30- to 60-second increments. Remove dried leaves from oven and allow to cool slightly. Discard any leaves that are not crisp. With your hands crumble suitable leaves onto waxed paper.*

4. *When crumbled leaves are completely cooled, crease waxed paper and funnel dried leaves into clean, dry containers. Close lids tightly and label each container with name of herb and date of drying. Store dried herbs in a cool, dark, dry location.*

CHUNKY FRESH TOMATO SAUCE

Use your garden tomatoes to prepare this delicious tomato sauce. It keeps in the refrigerator 1 or 2 days or in the freezer up to 6 months. Place a container of the sauce in a basket with fresh pasta, a loaf of Italian bread, and a bottle of red wine for a welcome gift.

> 2 cups ripe tomatoes, seeded and chopped
> 1 medium onion, chopped
> 1 green bell pepper, chopped
> 2 tablespoons chopped parsley
> 2 teaspoons chopped fresh basil or ¾ teaspoon dried basil
> 1½ teaspoons fresh oregano or ½ teaspoon dried oregano
> ½ teaspoon each salt and freshly ground pepper
> 1 can (6 oz) tomato paste

1. In a 3-quart microwave-safe casserole, combine tomatoes, onion, bell pepper, and parsley. Microwave on high (100%) until vegetables are soft (4 to 6 minutes).

2. Add basil, oregano, salt, ground pepper, and tomato paste; stir to blend. Microwave on high until hot (2 to 3 minutes). Let cool, then ladle into storage container, cover, and refrigerate.

Makes about 3½ cups.

ITALIAN MARINATED MOZZARELLA

Jars of these tasty little cheese cubes make wonderful gifts. They are good served on an antipasto tray or added to a tossed salad.

> 16 ounces mozzarella cheese, cut into ¾-inch cubes
> 1½ cups olive oil
> ½ cup dry red wine
> 3 cloves garlic, minced
> 2 tablespoons Italian seasoning
> 6 drops hot-pepper sauce
> 1 red bell pepper, chopped
> 1 tablespoon chopped parsley

1. Place cheese in a widemouthed 1½-quart jar with lid; set aside.

2. In a 4-cup microwave-safe measure, combine oil, wine, garlic, Italian seasoning, hot-pepper sauce, and bell pepper. Microwave on high (100%) until hot (3 to 5 minutes), stirring once. Let cool to room temperature, then stir in parsley.

3. Pour oil mixture over reserved cheese cubes; cover and shake to mix. Allow to stand in refrigerator 1 week, shaking occasionally.

4. With a slotted spoon remove cheese cubes from marinade and divide among decorative glass containers with lids. Fill each container almost to the top with marinade. Cover and label containers; store in refrigerator. Cheese cubes will keep refrigerated up to 4 weeks.

Makes 4 cups.

ZIPPY BARBECUE SAUCE

Here is the perfect hostess gift when you are invited to a summer barbecue. It is terrific brushed on ribs, chicken, or burgers while they are being broiled. The sauce can be made ahead and stored in the refrigerator. For long storage, place it in sterilized jars and process in a boiling water bath (see page 122).

> 2 cups chili sauce
> ½ cup lemon juice
> 1 medium onion, finely chopped
> ½ cup firmly packed brown sugar
> ¼ cup butter or margarine
> 2 tablespoons Worcestershire sauce
> 1½ teaspoons salt
> 1 teaspoon paprika
> ½ teaspoon cayenne pepper

Sterilize jars if using a boiling water bath. Meanwhile, in a 2-quart microwave-safe casserole, combine all ingredients. Microwave on high (100%) until mixture boils (3 to 5 minutes). Stir, then microwave again on high until mixture boils 1 minute. Let cool, then transfer to clean glass jars, cover, and store in refrigerator. The barbecue sauce will keep refrigerated up to 1 month. For longer storage, process 20 minutes in a boiling water bath.

Makes 4 half-pints.

MEXICAN SALSA

This spicy salsa is delicious served with tacos, eggs, or hamburgers. Make up a taco kit and pack all the necessary ingredients in a basket, including a jar of this tangy homemade sauce.

> 3 cups ripe tomatoes, washed, seeded, and chopped
> 2 jalapeño chiles seeded and chopped, or 1 can (4 oz) jalapeño chiles
> 1 tablespoon red wine vinegar
> 2 teaspoons chopped cilantro
> 1 teaspoon ground cumin
> ¼ teaspoon cayenne pepper

1. In a 3-quart microwave-safe casserole, combine all ingredients. Microwave on high (100%) until tomatoes are slightly soft (3 to 5 minutes), stirring once.

2. Let salsa cool to room temperature. Ladle into jars or other containers, cover, and store in refrigerator overnight before using. Salsa will keep up to 1 month refrigerated.

Makes 1½ cups.

SPICY CITRUS JELLY

Pack English muffins or biscuits in a pretty basket with this spicy jelly for a special breakfast treat. Note that the jelly jars should be sterilized before being filled and the filled jars should be processed in a boiling water bath (see page 122).

> 2 tablespoons grated orange rind
> 1 tablespoon grated lemon rind
> 1½ teaspoons whole allspice
> 2 teaspoons whole cloves
> 2 cups orange juice
> ½ cup lemon juice
> 1 package (1¾ oz) powdered pectin
> 4 cinnamon sticks (3 in. each)
> 3 cups sugar

1. Sterilize 4 half-pint jelly jars. Meanwhile combine orange rind, lemon rind, allspice, and cloves and tie in a cheesecloth bag.

2. In a 4-quart microwave-safe casserole, combine orange juice, lemon juice, and pectin. Add spice bag and cinnamon sticks. Cover and microwave on high (100%) until boiling rapidly (6 to 8 minutes), stirring every 2 minutes.

3. Add sugar. Microwave on high until mixture boils (6 to 8 minutes). Stir, then microwave again on high until mixture boils 1 minute. Remove spice bag; skim off foam. Remove cinnamon sticks from liquid and place 1 in each of the 4 sterilized jars. Pour jelly into jars to within ¼ inch of rim. Cover jars and process 5 minutes in boiling water bath.

Makes 4 half-pints.

SWEET HOT DOG RELISH

Your homemade relish will be a welcome gift for hot dogs or hamburgers cooked on the grill. If the condiment will be stored longer than 1 month in the refrigerator, place relish in sterilized jars and process in a boiling water bath (see page 122).

> 2 *cups chopped tomatoes (2 or 3 large tomatoes)*
> 1 *cup chopped green bell pepper*
> ½ *cup chopped onion*
> 1 *cup applesauce*
> 1 *cup sugar*
> 1 *teaspoon celery seed*
> ½ *teaspoon dry mustard*
> ½ *teaspoon ground cinnamon*

1. Sterilize jars if using a boiling water bath. Meanwhile in a 3-quart microwave-safe casserole, combine tomatoes, bell pepper, onion, and applesauce. Microwave on high (100%) until pepper and onion are soft (5 to 7 minutes).

2. Stir in sugar, celery seed, mustard, and cinnamon. Microwave on high until mixture boils and thickens (4 to 6 minutes), stirring once every minute. Relish will continue to thicken as it stands.

3. Ladle relish into clean jars. Cover, label, and store in the refrigerator. Relish will keep refrigerated up to 1 month. For longer storage, process 10 minutes in a boiling water bath.

Makes 3 half-pints.

SAVORIES

Attractively packaged, tasty nibbles such as these will be welcome gifts for any hostess.

CHEESE SQUARES

If you give these nibbles as a gift to a microwave cook, insert a note that suggests reheating in the microwave in a napkin-lined basket for 30 to 60 seconds on high (100%). These squares are delicious served with salad or soup.

> 1¼ *cups flour*
> 1½ *teaspoons salt*
> ½ *teaspoon dried basil*
> ½ *cup butter or margarine*
> 1 *egg yolk*
> ⅓ *cup grated Parmesan cheese*
> ½ *teaspoon paprika*

1. In a medium bowl combine flour, 1 teaspoon of the salt, and basil. Cut in butter until mixture is crumbly. Sprinkle with 4 tablespoons tap water and mix until flour is moistened and begins to form a ball. Wrap dough in waxed paper and chill 1 hour.

2. Divide dough in half; enclose half in waxed paper and refrigerate until used. On a pastry cloth or sheet of waxed paper, roll other half into a 10-inch square, taking care to make edges even.

3. Beat egg yolk with 1 teaspoon tap water. Brush on rolled dough. Combine cheese, the remaining ½ teaspoon salt, and paprika; sprinkle half of mixture on dough. Cut into 2-inch squares. Place 12 to 14 squares in a circle on a microwave-safe plate. Microwave on medium (50%) until surface appears dry and squares are golden (3 to 4 minutes). Let cool on a wire rack. Repeat with remaining dough. Store crackers tightly covered.

Makes about 40 squares.

PEAR CHUTNEY

Pack this tasty chutney into decorative jars or spoon it into a serving dish to accompany roast lamb, pork, or ham. For long storage, place the chutney in sterilized jars and process 15 minutes in a boiling water bath (see page 122).

> ¾ *cup white vinegar*
> 2 *cups sugar*
> 4 *large firm Bartlett pears, peeled, cored, and chopped*
> 1 *large onion, coarsely chopped*
> 1 *cup golden raisins*
> 1 *tablespoon ground ginger*
> 1 *clove garlic, minced*

1. Sterilize jars if using a boiling water bath. Meanwhile in a 4-quart microwave-safe casserole, combine vinegar and sugar. Cover and microwave on high (100%) until mixture boils (6 to 8 minutes).

2. Add pears, onion, raisins, ginger, and garlic. Cover and microwave on high until onion and pear are transparent (8 to 10 minutes).

3. Spoon chutney into jars or other containers, cover, and store in refrigerator. Chutney will keep refrigerated up to 1 month. For longer storage, fill jars to within ½ inch of rim, cover, and process 15 minutes in a boiling water bath.

Makes 4 half-pints.

BOILING WATER BATH

To lengthen the shelf life of food gifts, some recipes recommend water bath processing. Start by selecting the correct size canning jars with lids. Run the jars through a complete dishwasher cycle or wash them in soapy water and scald them with boiling water to sterilize. Then proceed as follows.

3. *With a pair of tongs, lower filled jars into water bath. Allow water to return to a boil, then process jars for time given in recipe.*

1. *Fill water bath canner or large stockpot with enough water to cover jars so that the surface is ½ inch above jar tops. Bring water to a boil. Meanwhile pack food into sterilized jars, leaving ¼ to ½ inch space below jar rims for expansion.*

2. *Insert clean plastic knife or wooden spoon handle into jars to remove air bubbles from food and liquid. Wipe rims with a clean damp cloth, then screw lids on firmly.*

4. *With a pair of tongs, remove processed jars from boiling water bath and place them several inches apart on a towel-covered counter. Allow jars to cool completely. Check seals on cooled jars to be sure the centers of the lids are slightly concave, indicating that a vacuum has been created. (If centers of lids are not concave, store jars in refrigerator for immediate use.) Label each jar to be stored with name of food and date of processing. Store jars in a cool, dark, dry location.*

SPICED APPLE RINGS

Stack these apple rings in canning jars or decorative jelly glasses. For storage longer than 2 weeks, place apple rings in sterilized jars and process in a boiling water bath according to photographs at left. The spiced apples are a delicious garnish with roast pork, ham, or chicken. The red food color gives the apple rings a festive look, but it may be omitted, if desired.

- 1 cup rosé wine
- ½ cup apple juice
- ½ cup sugar
- ¾ teaspoon ground cinnamon
- ¼ teaspoon ground allspice
- 1 teaspoon lemon juice
- ¼ teaspoon red food color (optional)
- 3 medium-sized red cooking apples (unpeeled) such as Rome Beauty or McIntosh

1. Sterilize jars if using a boiling water bath. Meanwhile in a 4-quart microwave-safe casserole, combine wine, apple juice, sugar, cinnamon, allspice, lemon juice, and food color, if used. Cover and microwave on high (100%) until mixture boils (5 to 8 minutes). Stir, then microwave again on high until mixture boils 2 minutes.

2. Wash and core apples. (Leaving peels on helps slices hold their shape.) Slice cored apples crosswise into ¼-inch-thick rings. Add half of rings to boiling liquid and microwave on high until rings are crisp-tender (2 to 3 minutes), stirring once. Remove cooked rings to a plate with a slotted spoon and repeat with remaining rings.

3. Stack cooked apple rings in wide-mouthed canning jars or jelly glasses. Fill jars almost to rims with cooking liquid. Cover and label jars; store in refrigerator. Spiced apples will keep refrigerated up to 2 weeks. For longer storage, process 10 minutes in a boiling water bath.

Makes 2 half-pints.

SPICED WALNUTS

For a quick, last-minute gift, pile these toasted nuts in a paper-doily-lined tin and tie with a pretty ribbon.

- 2 cups large walnut pieces
- ¼ cup sugar
- 2 teaspoons ground cinnamon
- ½ teaspoon ground allspice
- ¼ teaspoon ground nutmeg
- ¼ teaspoon ground cloves
- 2 tablespoons butter or margarine

1. Place walnuts in a 4-quart microwave-safe baking dish. Microwave on high (100%) until nuts are toasted (5 to 7 minutes), stirring twice and watching to prevent overbrowning.

2. Meanwhile, in a small bowl combine sugar, cinnamon, allspice, nutmeg, and cloves; set aside.

3. Stir butter into hot walnuts and toss until butter is melted and nuts are evenly coated. Add spice mixture and toss to coat all nuts. Turn coated nuts out onto waxed paper and let cool completely. Store in tightly covered container.

Makes 2 cups.

LEMON CURD

The English serve this thick lemon cream on toast, scones, or biscuits at teatime—a suggestion you could pass along on a gift tag. It is also good spooned into tart shells for dessert.

- 3 eggs
- 1¼ cups sugar
- 2 tablespoons finely grated lemon rind
- ⅓ cup lemon juice
- 4 tablespoons unsalted butter

1. In a 2-quart microwave-safe casserole, whip eggs until thick and lemon colored. Stir in sugar and lemon rind. Microwave on medium (50%) until lemon mixture is warm and sugar is dissolved (2 to 3 minutes), stirring once.

2. Add lemon juice and butter, stirring rapidly to mix. Microwave on medium-low (30%) until mixture is hot and slightly thickened (4 to 6 minutes), stirring twice. Let cool.

3. Ladle into jars or containers with lids, cover, and store in the refrigerator. The curd will keep refrigerated up to 3 weeks.

Makes 2 cups.

Bring out the best tea china and prepare your favorite scones to serve with Lemon Curd, a traditional English teatime offering. If you love lemon meringue pie, you'll appreciate this thick lemony cream as a delicious alternative to jam.

U.S. MEASURE AND METRIC MEASURE CONVERSION CHART

	Formulas for Exact Measures				Rounded Measures for Quick Reference		
	Symbol	**When you know:**	**Multiply by:**	**To find:**			
Mass (Weight)	oz	ounces	28.35	grams	1 oz		= 30 g
	lb	pounds	0.45	kilograms	4 oz		= 115 g
	g	grams	0.035	ounces	8 oz		= 225 g
	kg	kilograms	2.2	pounds	16 oz	= 1 lb	= 450 g
					32 oz	= 2 lb	= 900 g
					36 oz	= 2¼ lb	= 1,000g (1 kg)
Volume	tsp	teaspoons	5.0	milliliters	¼ tsp	= 1/24 oz	= 1 ml
	tbsp	tablespoons	15.0	milliliters	½ tsp	= 1/12 oz	= 2 ml
	fl oz	fluid ounces	29.57	milliliters	1 tsp	= ⅙ oz	= 5 ml
	c	cups	0.24	liters	1 tbsp	= ½ oz	= 15 ml
	pt	pints	0.47	liters	1 c	= 8 oz	= 250 ml
	qt	quarts	0.95	liters	2 c (1 pt)	= 16 oz	= 500 ml
	gal	gallons	3.785	liters	4 c (1 qt)	= 32 oz	= 1 liter
	ml	milliliters	0.034	fluid ounces	4 qt (1 gal)	= 128 oz	= 3¾ liter
Length	in.	inches	2.54	centimeters	⅜ in.	= 1 cm	
	ft	feet	30.48	centimeters	1 in.	= 2.5 cm	
	yd	yards	0.9144	meters	2 in.	= 5 cm	
	mi	miles	1.609	kilometers	2½ in.	= 6.5 cm	
	km	kilometers	0.621	miles	12 in. (1 ft)	= 30 cm	
	m	meters	1.094	yards	1 yd	= 90 cm	
	cm	centimeters	0.39	inches	100 ft	= 30 m	
					1 mi	= 1.6 km	
Temperature	°F	Fahrenheit	5/9 (after subtracting 32)	Celsius	32°F	= 0°C	
					68°F	= 20°C	
	°C	Celsius	9/5 (then add 32)	Fahrenheit	212°F	= 100°C	
Area	in.^{2}	square inches	6.452	square centimeters	1 in.^{2}	= 6.5 cm^2	
	ft^2	square feet	929.0	square centimeters	1 ft^2	= 930 cm^2	
	yd^2	square yards	8361.0	square centimeters	1 yd^2	= 8360 cm^2	
	a.	acres	0.4047	hectares	1 a.	= 4050 m^2	